The ABC of Caribbean Cookery

Kathy Janzan

CARIBBEAN

© Copyright text Kathy Janzan 1994
© Copyright illustrations Macmillan Education Ltd 1994

All rights reserved. No reproduction, copy or transmission of this publication may be made without written permission.

No paragraph of this publication may be reproduced, copied or transmitted save with written permission or in accordance with the provisions of the Copyright, Designs and Patents Act 1988, or under the terms of any licence permitting limited copying issued by the Copyright Licensing Agency, 90 Tottenham Court Road, London W1P 9HE.

Any person who does any unauthorised act in relation to this publication may be liable to criminal prosecution and civil claims for damages.

First published 1994 by
MACMILLAN EDUCATION LTD
London and Basingstoke
Companies and representatives throughout the world

ISBN 0–333–59860–1

11 10 9   8   7   6   5   4   3   2
06 05 04 03 02 01 00 99 98 97

This book is printed on paper suitable for recycling and made from fully managed and sustained forest sources.

Printed in Hong Kong

A catalogue record for this book is available from the British Library.

Colour photographs of recipes provided by the author.

Contents

Introduction	v
Map of the Caribbean Islands	vi
Tables of equivalent measures	viii
A to Z of recipes, Caribbean ingredients and Island notes	1
Suggested menus	117
Index	118

DEDICATION

This is for Salina.

INTRODUCTION

Christopher Colombus' successful landfall in the Windward and Leeward Islands of the Caribbean Sea around 1492, led the way for Europeans to follow in his footsteps. The islands were ripe for possession and exploitation for profit, much to the detriment of the indigenous population, the Amerindians, who were rapidly exterminated. Over the next five centuries the present population of the region was imported from the far-flung corners of the world and now all evidence of its Pre-Colombian past has virtually been eradicated.

Today, descendants of African, English, French, Dutch, Scottish, Syrian, Lebanese, Chinese, Irish and Nova Scotian are examples of the huge melting pot of cultures present in these islands. Similarly, the majority of the foods and crops were, and still are imported.

The culmination of these different peoples and cultures expresses itself most obviously in the food – the variety of ingredients, methods of preparation and adventurous use of herbs and spices. West Indian society is strongly family orientated and food plays an important role in family life. Much time is spent preparing food for family gatherings, village cook-outs and National holidays and festivals. Consequently, a whole array of delicious dishes are created from the natural and plentiful ingredients that surround these people – exotic fruits and vegetables grow in untamed profusion and the seas abound with seemingly endless supplies of fish and shellfish. Sadly, visitors to the Caribbean often leave feeling that they have missed out on traditional West Indian cuisine as many restaurants cater for the American and European palate.

During the seven years that I spent cooking on charter yachts in the Caribbean, I was very aware of the importance of 'tantalizing' the guests' palate with a range of tastes and smells from a variety of foods they might not have encountered before. Not only did they sample the more traditional fare but were also introduced to numerous inventions of my own. During our cruises up and down the islands, from the American and British Virgin Islands in the north to Grenada in the south, I would often take the guests on a shopping expedition. Mostly, they had never experienced such disorder, noise and profusion of colours and smells; being used to the hushed, piped-music atmosphere of the supermarkets back home with orderly rows of plump, too-perfect fruits and vegetables. It was quite an education for them!

Today, people are more adventurous in their approach to food and want to experiment with recipes from around the world. Now that so many of these ingredients are available outside of the Caribbean I hope that you will use this book to add fire and spice, colour and flair to your own cooking.

Kathy Janzan 1994

Greater Antilles

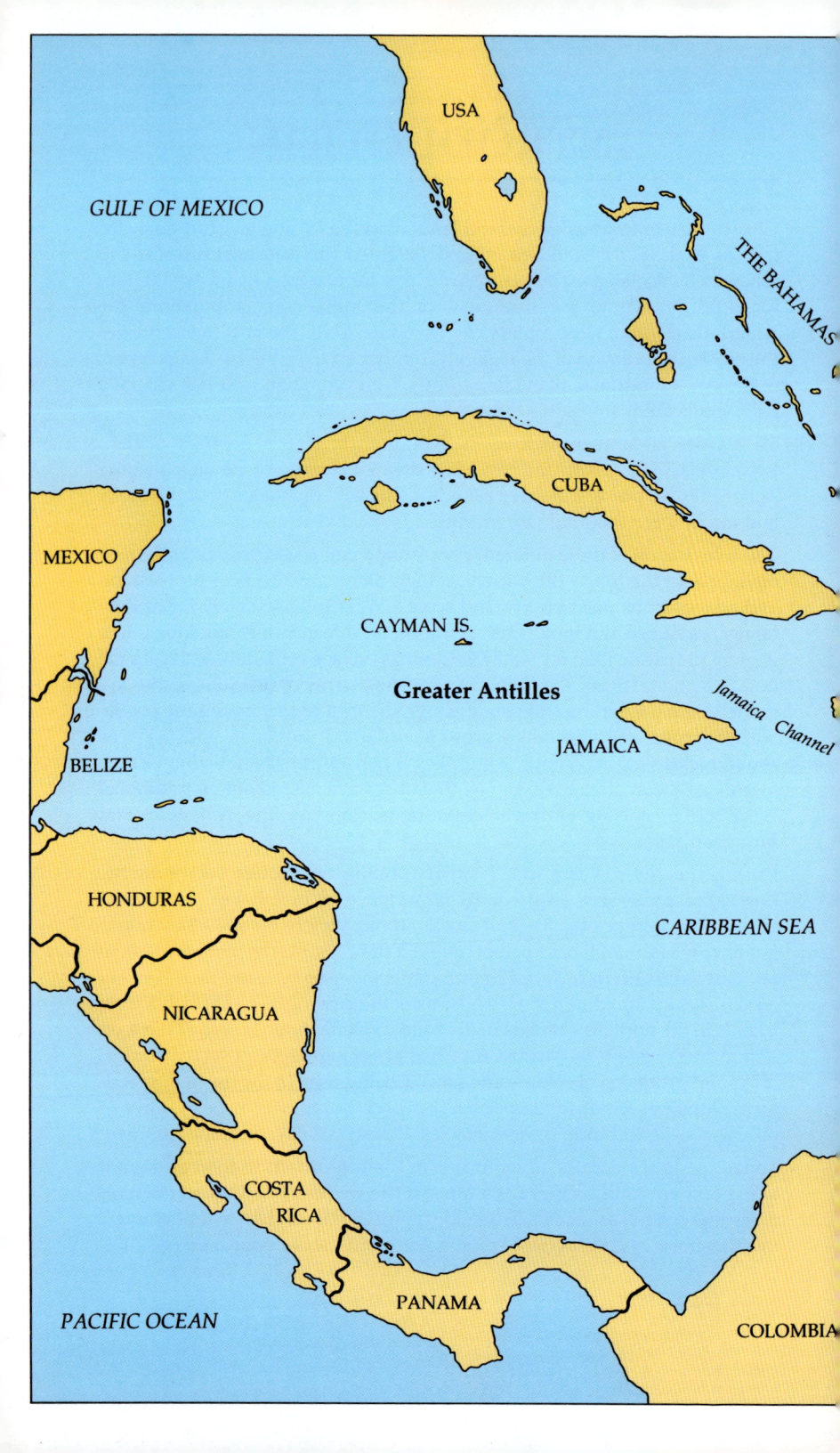

ATLANTIC OCEAN

HAITI
DOMINICAN REPUBLIC
VIRGIN IS.
Virgin Gorda
Tortola
St Thomas
St John
ANGUILLA
ST MARTIN
ST MAARTEN
St Bartélemy
PUERTO RICO
St Croix
ST KITTS
ANTIGUA
NEVIS
BARBUDA
MONTSERRAT
GUADELOUPE
DOMINICA
MARTINIQUE
ST LUCIA
BARBADOS
ST VINCENT
Bequia
Carriacou
GRENADA

Leeward Islands
Lesser Antilles
Windward Islands

ARUBA
CURACAO
BONAIRE

TOBAGO
TRINIDAD

VENEZUELA
GUYANA

TABLES OF EQUIVALENT MEASURES

FLUID EQUIVALENTS

8 pints = 1 gallon
1 pint = 20 fluid oz = 2 cups = 568 ml = 32 tablespoons
¼ pint = 5 fluid oz = ½ cup = 142 ml = 8 tablespoons
1 tablespoon = ½ fluid oz
1 teaspoon = ⅙ fluid oz

SOLID EQUIVALENTS

16 oz = 454 g
8 oz = 227 g
4 oz = 113 g
1 oz = 28 g

APPROXIMATE OVEN TEMPERATURE EQUIVALENTS

Very low oven   = 250°F = 130°C = Gas Mark ½
Low oven   = 300°F = 150°C = Gas Mark 2
Moderate oven   = 350°F = 180°C = Gas Mark 4
Very hot oven   = 400°F = 200°C = Gas Mark 6
Extremely hot oven = 450°F = 230°C = Gas Mark 8

ACKEE (Akee)

The fruit of an evergreen tree introduced to Jamaica from West Africa. It is pear-shaped, reddish-yellow in colour and when ripe bursts open to display shiny black seeds covered by a creamy yellow flesh, which is the edible portion. This has a slightly lemony flavour and a texture similar to scrambled eggs. It is traditionally served with saltfish but is also delicious with shellfish or vegetables. It is now exported from Jamaica in tinned form.

ACKEE, MUSHROOM AND CHEESE SOUFFLÉ

To serve 6:

2 oz mushrooms, washed and thinly sliced

2½ oz butter (plus ½ tablespoon for greasing)

1 oz flour

⅓ pint milk

5 eggs, separated

3 oz cheddar cheese

½ teaspoon salt

Freshly ground black pepper

½ teaspoon Dijon mustard

12 oz can of ackees, drained and puréed

Heat the oven to 350°F and grease a 2½ pint soufflé dish with butter. In a small frying pan melt 1 oz of butter and lightly sauté the mushrooms until soft – finely mince them in a food processor. Melt the remaining 1½ oz of butter in a saucepan, sprinkle on the flour and cook, stirring, for 1 minute. Gradually add the milk, whisking continuously bring to the boil and thicken. Remove from the heat and allow to cool before adding the egg yolks, beating well. Add the cheese, salt and pepper to taste, mustard, mushroom and ackee purée. Whisk the egg whites to stiff peaks and fold gently into the mixture. Pour into the prepared soufflé dish and bake for 30–40 minutes until risen and golden brown. Serve immediately.

ALLSPICE

This should not be confused with a French spice mixture called 'Quatre Epices', or Four Spices. These red-brown berries harbour a rich combination of flavours of cinnamon, clove, nutmeg and juniper berries. Allspice can be used alone or in combination with other spices.

ANGUILLA

Anguilla is the Spanish name for eel and is a very apt name for this long, thin shaped island. Although it is low-lying and hence rather barren and scrubby, Anguilla has some of the most beautiful deserted sandy beaches. It is also famed for its scenic snorkling and diving and because of these factors houses several of the most exclusive resorts in the Caribbean. Charter yachts are not exactly unwelcome but anchorages and duration of stay are both limited.

ANTIGUA

An island of coral and volcanic creation, famed for its 365 beaches (one for each day of the year!!) and its succulent Antiguan black pineapple. Other local delicacies include pepperpot with fungi (cornmeal dumplings), saltfish and goatwater (a spicy goat stew). Of the Leeward and Windward islands, Antigua is probably one of the most developed for tourism. The north-west end of the island is known as 'hotel row'. English Harbour on the southern end of the island was the safe harbour for the British fleet under the command of Admiral Lord Horatio Nelson. Nelson's Dockyard contains several well restored buildings now utilised as bars, restaurants, museums, boutiques and other small businesses. The island is the centre of the Caribbean yacht charter community and host to the world famous Antigua Sailing Week, held every April/May. Yachts from all over the world partake in a week of vigorous racing and partying.

AVOCADO AND BASIL SOUP

To serve 4:

1½ oz butter

1 small onion, peeled and finely chopped

1 oz plain flour

1 pint chicken stock

1 large ripe avocado, peeled, pitted and the flesh roughly chopped

2 teaspoons lemon juice

Black pepper, to taste

8 tablespoons milk

8 tablespoons cream

2 tablespoons chopped fresh basil leaves

Melt the butter in a large saucepan. Add the onion and fry for 2–3 minutes, until soft and transparent. Add the flour and cook for 1 minute. Gradually add the stock and bring to the boil. Add the avocado, lemon juice and pepper. Simmer, covered for 8–10 minutes. Cool and then liquidise and turn into a bowl. Add the milk and cream, cover and refrigerate. Just before serving add the basil. If a stronger basil flavour is desired, add the basil to the soup 2–3 hours before serving.

Avocado lime mousse with chutney chicken salad

AVOCADO AND CRAB SALAD
with a piquant tomato sauce

To serve 4:

2 ripe avocados, peeled, pitted and sliced

6 oz crab meat ('crab sticks' may be substituted)

Finely grated peel and juice of a fresh lime

For sauce:
4 tablespoons mayonnaise

4 tablespoons tomato ketchup

1 teaspoon mustard

1 teaspoon Worcester sauce

3 drops hot sauce or to taste

1 teaspoon horseradish sauce

Blend together all the ingredients for the sauce. Drizzle the slices of avocado with the lime juice to prevent discolouration. Arrange the avocado slices in a decorative fan shape on a serving plate. Roughly chop the crab meat and toss gently with the sauce. Place a small mound of the dressed crab meat at the apex of the fan. Garnish with lime peel, tomato quarters and cucumber swirls.

AVOCADO LIME MOUSSE
with chutney chicken salad

To serve 4:

For chutney chicken salad:
6 tablespoons mayonnaise

2 teaspoons lime juice

¼ teaspoon salt

3 tablespoons finely chopped mango chutney

1 teaspoon curry powder

1½ lb diced cooked chicken

For avocado lime mousse:
3 oz lime flavoured gelatin

6 tablespoons boiling water

6 tablespoons dry white wine

3 oz cream cheese

2 ripe avocados, peeled, pitted and mashed

1 tablespoon lime juice

1 oz thinly sliced green onion

2 oz finely diced celery

½ teaspoon salt

4 tablespoons mayonnaise

Lettuce leaves and cherry tomatoes to garnish

Blend together the ingredients for the chutney dressing and pour over the chicken. Combine well, cover and chill. Dissolve the gelatin in the boiling water, stir in the wine and set aside to thicken. Beat the cream cheese until smooth, add the mashed avocados, mayonnaise, lime juice, onion, celery, salt and gelatin mixture. Pour into an oiled 1 quart bundt mould. Cover and chill for at least 3 hours. When it has set, unmould and pile the chutney chicken into the centre. Garnish with the lettuce and cherry tomatoes.

(Illustrated on page 3)

AVOCADO AND PAPAYA SALAD

To serve 4:

2 avocados

1 large ripe papaya

2 tablespoons white wine vinegar

1 tablespoon fresh lime juice

2 tablespoons olive oil

½ teaspoon mustard

Black pepper to taste

Lime and parsley to garnish

Cut the avocado in half, remove the stone and using a melon-baller remove as much of the flesh as possible. Cut the papaya in half, remove the seeds. Use the melon-baller to remove all the flesh. Arrange the balls decoratively in individual glass dishes. Whisk together the vinegar, lime juice, olive oil, mustard and black pepper and drizzle over the avocado and papaya. Garnish with a quarter of lime and a sprig of parsley.

AVOCADO WITH SPINACH AND GARLIC MAYONNAISE

To serve 6:

3 ripe avocados, cut in half, peeled and pitted

8 oz fresh or frozen spinach, (if frozen, thawed and drained)

2 cloves garlic, peeled and chopped

1 tablespoon fresh lime juice

Hot sauce to taste

6 tablespoons mayonnaise

Parsley to garnish

Blanch fresh spinach in a saucepan of boiling water for 1 minute. **N.B.** The next stage is much easier if a food processor is used. Place the spinach, garlic, lime juice and hot sauce in a food processor and whizz to a smooth paste. Add the mayonnaise and whizz again. Scrape into a small bowl, cover and chill. Place the prepared avocados hole down on a serving dish, spoon the chilled sauce over and garnish with parsley.

Avocado and papaya salad

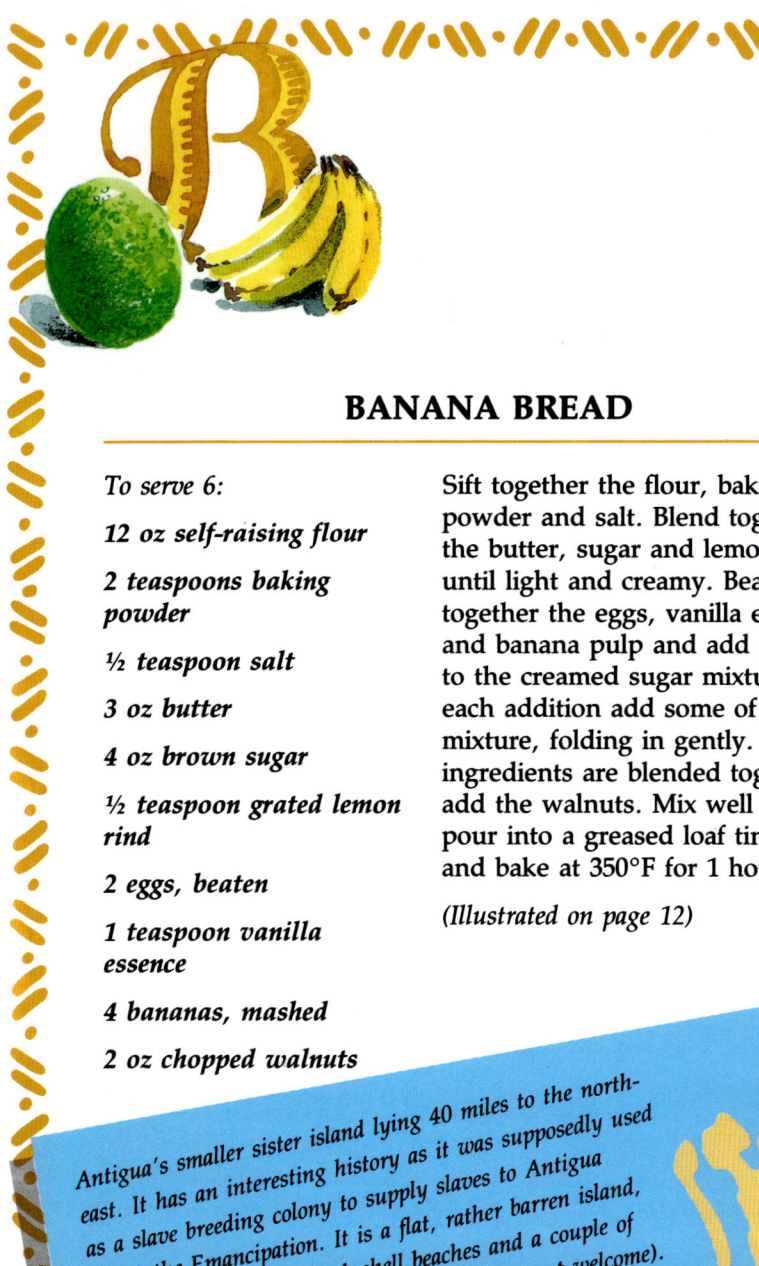

BANANA BREAD

To serve 6:

12 oz self-raising flour

2 teaspoons baking powder

½ teaspoon salt

3 oz butter

4 oz brown sugar

½ teaspoon grated lemon rind

2 eggs, beaten

1 teaspoon vanilla essence

4 bananas, mashed

2 oz chopped walnuts

Sift together the flour, baking powder and salt. Blend together the butter, sugar and lemon rind until light and creamy. Beat together the eggs, vanilla essence and banana pulp and add gradually to the creamed sugar mixture. After each addition add some of the flour mixture, folding in gently. When all ingredients are blended together add the walnuts. Mix well and pour into a greased loaf tin (8″ × 4″) and bake at 350°F for 1 hour.

(Illustrated on page 12)

BARBUDA

Antigua's smaller sister island lying 40 miles to the north-east. It has an interesting history as it was supposedly used as a slave breeding colony to supply slaves to Antigua before the Emancipation. It is a flat, rather barren island, with miles of deserted pink shell beaches and a couple of very exclusive resorts (unannounced visitors **not** welcome). In the central part of the island are caves with the remains of Carib Indian drawings. The local fishermen will take you across the Codrington lagoon to see the Frigate bird breeding colony.

SAUTÉED BANANAS WITH COCONUT CREAM

To serve 6:

Juice of 1 lime

4 oz butter

6 oz soft brown sugar

6 bananas, peeled and cut into ½" slices

8 tablespoons cream

4 oz dessicated coconut

Pinch of salt

Place the lime juice, butter and sugar in a large frying pan over a moderate heat, mixing well to melt the butter and dissolve the sugar. Add the bananas and cook over a high heat with the juice bubbling for 5 minutes. Stir gently. Turn into a shallow dish and leave to cool. To make the coconut cream, put the cream and coconut into a saucepan, bring to the boil and simmer for 5 minutes. Remove from the heat and add a pinch of salt. Allow to cool and then pour the liquid onto the bananas through a sieve, pressing the coconut with the back of a spoon. Leave to cool at room temperature.

BANANA COCONUT PUDDING

To serve 6:

1¼ pints water

2 tablespoons brown sugar

4 oz coconut cream

10 glacé cherries, roughly chopped

4 tablespoons sago

1 tablespoon white sugar

4 bananas, peeled and sliced

¼ pint evaporated milk

Pinch of salt

Bring 1 pint of water to the boil in a large saucepan. Add the sago, sugars and, stirring slowly, add the coconut cream and remaining water. Bring to the boil, stirring all the time. Reduce the heat and simmer until the sago is cooked. Add the bananas, cherries, evaporated milk and salt. Cook stirring gently for a further 5 minutes. Pour into a serving dish. Can be served hot or cold.

BANANA CREAM PIE

To serve 6:

1 packet of gingernut biscuits, ground to a fine powder

3 oz butter

3 oz brown sugar

½ pint milk

½ teaspoon vanilla essence

Zest of one orange

2 oz cornflour

3 bananas, peeled and sliced

8 tablespoons whipping cream

Melt the butter and add to the ground biscuits along with 1 oz of sugar. Press into a greased 7" pie dish. Chill until hard. Heat the milk in a small saucepan, add the vanilla essence, orange zest and 2 oz of brown sugar. Simmer for 3 minutes. Mix the cornflour with 2 tablespoons of milk. Bring the milk mixture to the boil and add the cornflour. Stir constantly and allow to thicken. Add to the biscuit base and allow to cool and set. Place a circle of greaseproof paper over the custard to prevent a skin forming. Arrange the banana slices decoratively on top of the custard. Whip the cream and pipe onto the bananas.

BANANA FLAMBÉ

To serve 4:

4 ripe bananas, peeled and sliced in two lengthways

4 oz butter

2 tablespoons brown sugar

4 tablespoons dark rum

Melt the butter in a frying pan and add the sugar. Stir until melted. Add the bananas and simmer gently in the syrup for 3–4 minutes. Turn the flame higher so that the syrup is bubbling, add the rum and ignite. Shake the pan so as to catch all the alcohol and burn it off. Serve immediately.

PAN-FRIED HONEY BANANAS

To serve 3:

3 ripe bananas

8 tablespoons orange juice

Honey to taste

1 teaspoon freshly grated ginger

2 teaspoons dessicated coconut

½ teaspoon ground cinnamon

Blend together the orange juice, honey and ginger. Place in a frying pan and heat through to simmering. Add the bananas, peeled and sliced in two lengthways, and cook gently until the sauce starts to thicken. Sprinkle over the coconut and cinnamon and serve immediately.

BARBADOS

The resort island of this part of the Caribbean is characterised by its vast geographical differences to the other islands. There are no volcanoes or rainforests and hardly any rivers. However, there are glorious white sand beaches and pleasantly rolling countryside with fields of sugar cane, brightly painted villages and flowering trees of bougainvillea and frangipani. This scene must have made the first British colonists feel less homesick. The local cuisine has distinction and flair: pudding and souse is a huge dish of pickled breadfruit, black pudding and pork; flying fish, the National emblem, is a speciality filleted, coated in flour and spices and fried; sea eggs, the roe of the white sea urchin; cou-cou, a starchy dish made from breadfruit or cornmeal; jug-jug, a poor man's haggis made from guinea corn.

Barbecue

*The Carib Indians used a **brabacot**, which was a platform of green sticks, animal hides and bones built over a fire and used to smoke-dry freshly caught game, before taking it back to camp. The Spanish adapted this name to barbacao and from this grew the art of barbecuing.*

CARIBBEAN BANANA SOUP

To serve 6:

6 bananas, peeled and mashed

2 pints vegetable stock

1 onion, peeled and finely chopped

1 green pepper, deseeded and finely chopped

2 cloves garlic, peeled and minced

2 tablespoons oil

4 oz grated coconut

⅔ pint milk

Place the stock and bananas in a large saucepan and bring to the boil. Simmer for 10 minutes. In another saucepan, heat the oil and fry the onion, green pepper and garlic until soft. Add the coconut and cook for 3 minutes, stirring gently. Add the coconut mixture to the bananas, season with salt and pepper and hot sauce if desired. Simmer for 30 minutes before serving.

Banana bread

ST BARTS

This small island is a Department of France and as such is very popular with well-to-do French and American families. It is actually St Barthélemy but the name is usually shortened to St Barts. Its French connections are very obvious in its excellent French and Creole restaurants. A surprising feature is its almost totally Caucasian population, due to the influx of escaped white slaves after neighbouring islands' emancipation.

BEAN AND CASHEW NUT SALAD

To serve 4:

8 oz can dark red kidney beans

8 oz can lima beans

8 oz can chick peas

4 tablespoons red wine vinegar

4 tablespoons olive oil

1 tablespoon tomato purée

1 teaspoon honey

3 drops hot sauce

1 teaspoon mustard

½ teaspoon Worcester sauce

1 teaspoon finely chopped basil

Black pepper to taste

2 oz freshly roasted cashew nuts

Wash and drain the beans and peas and mix together in a salad bowl. Whisk together all the other ingredients except the cashew nuts, pour over the beans and toss gently. Sprinkle the cashew nuts on top to serve.

CARIBBEAN BEEF

To serve 4:

1 lb minced beef

2 oz butter

3 tomatoes, peeled and roughly chopped

4 onions, peeled and sliced

1 clove garlic, peeled and minced

2 tablespoons sultanas

1 lb cooked rice

2 chillies, deseeded and finely chopped

4 oz salted peanuts

¼ teaspoon oregano

¼ teaspoon black pepper

Melt the butter in a heavy saucepan and add the garlic and onions. Fry for 1 minute until transparent. Add the minced beef and brown quickly; lower the heat and add the tomatoes, sultanas and chillies. Cover and cook over a low heat for approximately 40 minutes, stirring occasionally. Add the peanuts and rice and heat through for 5 minutes before serving.

WEST INDIAN BEEF

To serve 4:

1½ lb stewing steak, cut into 2" × 1" strips

2 onions, peeled and sliced

1 green chilli, deseeded and sliced

¼ teaspoon cayenne pepper

1 tablespoon flour

4 oz lean bacon strips

1 lb tomatoes, peeled and roughly chopped

¼ pint water

1 teaspoon oregano

½ teaspoon salt

Combine the oregano, cayenne and salt with the flour and coat the meat strips with this mixture. Place the stewing steak in a casserole. Remove the rind from the bacon and cut into 1" pieces and place on top of the meat. Lay the chilli and onions on top of the bacon. Combine the water and tomatoes and place this mixture on top of the onions. Cover and cook in an oven at 325°F for 1½ hours or until the meat is tender.

Serve with coconut rice (page 94).

West Indian beef with coconut rice

Breadfruit

The breadfruit tree is one of the tallest trees in the tropical rainforest. It has beautiful, large, glossy, heavily serrated dark green leaves. The 'fruit' is large, round and bright green in colour; it can reach up to 4 lbs in weight. The skin is tough and fibrous and covered with dimple-like pock marks. This delicious starchy vegetable can be substituted for potato, rice or pasta.

BREADFRUIT BAKED WHOLE

To serve 6:

1 breadfruit

Butter

Pierce the skin of the breadfruit in several places and either place over a barbecue grill or directly into the flaming embers of a wood fire. Leave for 45 minutes, turning occasionally. Break open and the vegetable is like hot, doughy bread. Serve with lashings of butter.

BREADFRUIT WITH GARLIC BUTTER

To serve 6:

1 breadfruit

6 cloves of garlic, peeled and minced

4 oz butter

Peel and slice the breadfruit into pieces approximately 3" long by ¼" thick. Place in a saucepan of boiling water for 3 minutes. Drain. Melt butter in a frying pan, add the garlic and cook until softened. Add the breadfruit and gently sauté until the breadfruit is cooked. Alternatively, arrange the breadfruit in a buttered ovenproof dish, pour over the garlic butter and cook in the oven at 400°F for about 20 minutes. Sprinkle with fresh parsley to serve.

Butternut

A type of squash very similar in taste and texture to pumpkin. This is a smaller, pear shaped vegetable with a tough, light brown skin and bright orange flesh. Its flavour is sweet and nutty.

BAKED BUTTERNUT SQUASH
with cinnamon

To serve 6:

3 medium butternuts, halved and deseeded

3 oz butter

3 teaspoons ground cinnamon

Black pepper to taste

2 rashers of streaky bacon cut into 6 pieces

Place ½ oz of butter into the well of each half of butternut. Sprinkle liberally with cinnamon and black pepper. Place one piece of bacon in each well. Bake at 400°F for approximately 45 minutes until the squash is tender.

Baked butternut squash with cinnamon

CURRIED CREAM OF BUTTERNUT AND LEEK SOUP

To serve 8:

4 oz butter

1 oz curry powder

6 oz chopped leeks, green and white parts

4 lb butternut squash, peeled, deseeded and cut into 1" pieces

3 pints chicken stock

¼ teaspoon thyme

Salt and pepper to taste

8 tablespoons cream

8 tablespoons milk

4 oz parmesan cheese, finely grated

Chopped chives or parsley to garnish

Melt the butter in a large pan, add the curry powder and cook for 1 minute. Add the leeks and cook, stirring, until soft. Stir in the squash and add the stock, thyme and salt and pepper. Simmer for 40 minutes or until the squash is tender. Place in a blender and liquidise until smooth. Return to a clean saucepan and add the milk and cream. Reheat (thin with a little more milk if desired). Serve hot, sprinkled with parmesan and chives or parsley.

BUTTERNUT SQUASH CASSEROLE

To serve 6:

1 lb butternut, peeled, deseeded and chopped into 1" pieces

1 medium onion, peeled and finely chopped

2 oz butter

8 oz fresh breadcrumbs

6 oz can concentrated cream of celery soup

6 tablespoons sour cream

Salt and pepper to taste

1 tablespoon chopped parsley

1 teaspoon rosemary

Melt the butter and sauté the onion until soft and transparent. Combine all other ingredients together with the onion and place in a greased casserole dish. Bake at 325°F for 45 minutes until the squash is tender and the top is crunchy.

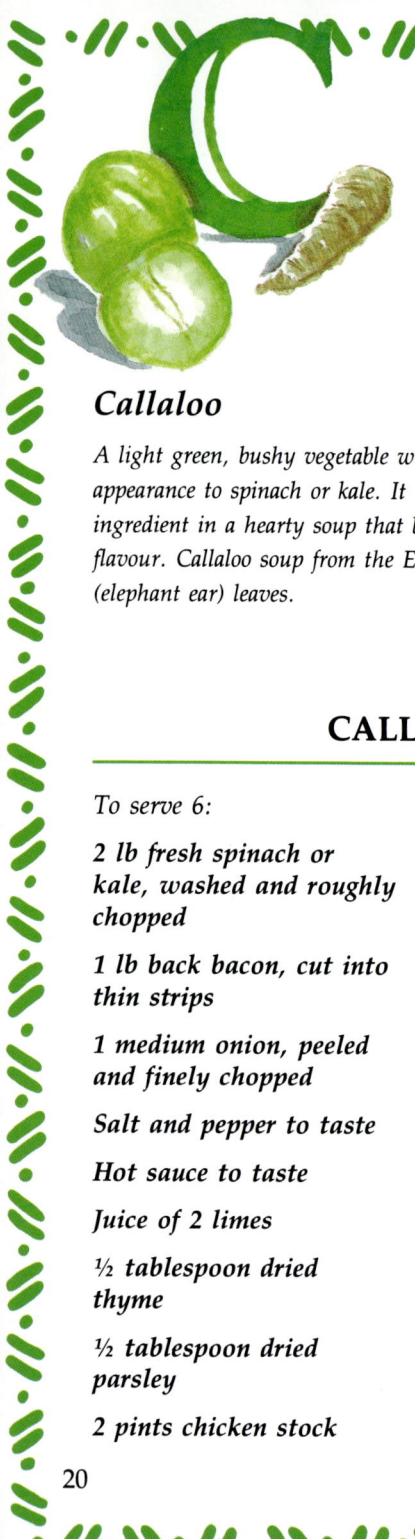

Callaloo

A light green, bushy vegetable with thin-veined leaves which is very similar in appearance to spinach or kale. It may also be known as bhaji. It is the main ingredient in a hearty soup that bears its name and imparts a lovely peppery flavour. Callaloo soup from the Eastern Caribbean is made with dasheen (elephant ear) leaves.

CALLALOO SOUP

To serve 6:

2 lb fresh spinach or kale, washed and roughly chopped

1 lb back bacon, cut into thin strips

1 medium onion, peeled and finely chopped

Salt and pepper to taste

Hot sauce to taste

Juice of 2 limes

½ tablespoon dried thyme

½ tablespoon dried parsley

2 pints chicken stock

Place the bacon in a heavy pan and sauté until the fat has been rendered, approximately 10 minutes. Drain off the fat, except for one tablespoon. Add the onions and sauté until transparent. Add half the spinach or kale, salt and pepper, hot sauce, lime juice, herbs and stock. When the first batch of spinach has wilted add the remainder. Cover and simmer for 30 minutes. Place in a blender and liquidise until smooth. Return to a clean pan, reheat and serve. This soup is one that benefits from a day in the fridge and is even better the next day.

(Illustrated on page 23)

CARROT AND GINGER SOUP

To serve 6:

3 oz butter

1 large onion, peeled and finely chopped

2 oz fresh ginger root, peeled and minced

2 cloves garlic, peeled and minced

1½ pints chicken stock

6 tablespoons dry white wine

2 lb carrots, peeled and sliced

2 tablespoons fresh lime juice

Pinch of ground cinnamon

Salt and pepper to taste

Cream and parsley to garnish

Melt the butter in a large pan, add the onion, ginger and garlic and sauté for 10 minutes. Add the carrots, stock and wine. Bring to the boil, reduce the heat and simmer for approximately 45 minutes or until the carrots are tender. Add the lime juice and cinnamon. Place in a blender and liquidise until smooth. Add salt and pepper to taste. Serve hot with a sprinkle of parsley and swirl of cream.

Cassava

A root vegetable originally cultivated by the Arawak Indians. It is also known as yucca or manioc. There are two varieties, sweet and bitter. The bitter cassava is considered poisonous before it is cooked and a special straining preparation must be performed to remove the toxins: pulp from the grated cassava is placed in a long, thin woven cylinder called a matapie, then hung and weighted. Stretching the weave of the cylinder forces out the poisonous juices and the pulp is then rendered harmless. It is used after it has been sundried, being made into meal and then bread.

CARIBBEAN CHICKEN SALAD

To serve 4:

4 chicken breasts, cooked and meat cut into bite-sized pieces

1 green pepper, deseeded and roughly chopped

3 sticks celery cut into ½" pieces

1 red apple cored and sliced

½ fresh pineapple, skinned and cut into chunks (alternatively the meat can be removed without damaging the skin and the shell can be used as a decorative serving dish)

1 fresh mango, peeled, pitted and cut into chunks

For dressing:
6 tablespoons mayonnaise

6 tablespoons sour cream

2 tablespoons coconut cream

1 tablespoon curry paste

1 tablespoon pineapple juice

Salt and pepper to taste

Mix together all the ingredients for the salad. Blend together the dressing ingredients and gently fold into the chicken mixture. Serve chilled on a bed of lettuce or in the half pineapple shell.

Callaloo soup

Caribbean chicken salad

CINNAMON CHICKEN WITH PLANTAINS

To serve 4:

1 large onion, peeled and finely chopped

4 chicken breasts

3 oz butter

2 tablespoons ground cinnamon

⅓ pint chicken stock

1 tablespoon brown sugar

Salt and pepper to taste

2 plantains, peeled and cut into 1" rounds

Place onion, chicken, butter, cinnamon, stock and salt and pepper in a large saucepan and heat gently until the butter has melted. Bring to the boil, cover and simmer for 5 minutes. Heat oven to 400°F and warm an ovenproof casserole dish. Remove the chicken from the pan and place in the casserole dish. Add the sugar and plantains to the pan and cook for 5 minutes, stirring to dissolve the sugar. Add this mixture to the chicken and cook in the oven for 45 minutes or until the chicken is tender, basting frequently. Strain all the liquid from the casserole into a saucepan (keep the chicken and plantains warm) and boil vigorously until the sauce is thick and syrupy. Spoon this over the chicken just before serving.

BARBECUED CHICKEN WINGS

To serve 4:

1 lb chicken wings

Salt and pepper

4 tablespoons tomato ketchup

1 tablespoon Worcester sauce

½ tablespoon mustard

1 tablespoon brown sugar

1 tablespoon vinegar

1 teaspoon hot sauce, or to taste

Douse the chicken wings liberally with salt and pepper. Blend together all the other ingredients and toss the chicken wings in this sauce, making sure that they are evenly coated. Place wings in a single layer on an oiled baking tray and cook in a hot oven, 425°F for 25–30 minutes or until the wings are crisp and slightly burnt on the edges. These are also very good cooked on a barbecue grill.

Barbecued chicken wings

CHICKEN BREASTS STUFFED WITH BANANA
with a mango sauce

To serve 4:

4 boneless chicken breasts

2 bananas, peeled

¼ pint chicken stock or white wine

1 fresh mango, peeled and flesh puréed

¼ pint white wine

¼ pint sour cream

Juice of half a lime

Lime peel to garnish

Beat each chicken breast between two pieces of waxed paper until they are approximately ¼" thick. Rub one side with a small amount of black pepper. Place half a banana in the centre and roll the flesh over it, securing with a wooden toothpick. Place all the chicken breasts edge down on a greased baking dish. Pour over the wine or stock, cover and bake at 350°F for 40–45 minutes or until the chicken juices run clear.

To make the sauce: heat together the mango purée and cooking liquid for 3 minutes, simmering gently. Add the sour cream and blend together well. Add the lime juice, heat through and pour over the cooked chicken breasts when serving. Garnish with decorative swirls of lime peel.

CHICKEN SATE

To serve 4:

2 boneless chicken breasts

Juice and grated rind of one lime

For sauce:
2 tablespoons smooth peanut butter

1 tablespoon soy sauce

½ teaspoon hot sauce

½ teaspoon ground ginger

1 tablespoon honey

1 teaspoon tomato purée

1 teaspoon oil

Combine all the ingredients for the sauce. Cut the chicken breasts into bite-sized pieces and marinade in the lime juice for 2 hours. After this time skewer the meat onto metal skewers and dip into the sate sauce. Sprinkle with the lime rind and grill under a hot grill or on a barbecue grill, turning to prevent burning. Serve with lemon and garlic rice, page 95.

Chicken sate with lemon and garlic rice

HONEY CHICKEN
with lemon and garlic stuffing

To serve 4:

4 boneless chicken breasts

1 tablespoon honey

1 teaspoon white wine vinegar

4 oz breadcrumbs

1 oz butter

4 cloves garlic, peeled and crushed

Juice and grated rind of 1 lemon

Pinch of paprika

Salt and pepper to taste

Beat each chicken breast between two sheets of waxed paper until they are ¼" thick. Combine the breadcrumbs, melted butter, lemon, garlic, paprika and salt and pepper until they are bound together. Divide the stuffing into four and place one quarter on each chicken breast. Roll over the edges to seal the stuffing in, using a wooden toothpick if necessary to secure. Place the chicken breasts on a well oiled baking tray. Score the surface of the chicken lightly. Combine the honey and vinegar and brush this mixture onto the chicken. Bake at 350°F for 35–45 minutes or until the chicken juices run clear.

CHICKEN, AVOCADO AND MANGO SALAD
with a lime – hazelnut dressing

To serve 4:

2 pints lightly salted water

4 chicken breasts, skinned and boned

1 head chicory, washed and trimmed

2 small endives, washed and trimmed

2 ripe avocados, peeled, pitted and cut into ¼" slices

2 ripe mangoes, peeled, pitted and cut into ¼" slices

1 large red pepper, deseeded and finely chopped

For lime – hazelnut dressing:
3 oz hazelnuts

5 tablespoons olive oil

5 tablespoons fresh lime juice

2 tablespoons fresh parsley, chopped

¼ teaspoon salt

Pinch ground cumin

Freshly ground black pepper

To make the lime – hazelnut dressing: heat the oven to 350°F and toast the hazelnuts in a shallow baking pan, shaking occasionally until the skins are well browned and the nut meats are pale brown, approximately 15 minutes. Rub the nuts through a coarse sieve to remove most of the skins. Grind the nuts in a food processor. Whisk together the oil, lime juice, parsley, salt, cumin and pepper to taste; pour into a jar. Add the ground hazelnuts and shake until well blended.
Boil the salted water in a heavy saucepan. Add the chicken breasts and simmer until the chicken is cooked. Remove with a slotted spoon and allow to cool.
Meanwhile prepare the remaining ingredients: Roughly shred the chickory and toss with 2 tablespoons of dressing. Divide equally between four salad plates. Toss the shredded endives with 2 tablespoons of dressing and place on top of the chicory. Cut the chicken breasts diagonally into ¼" slices, toss with 2 tablespoons of dressing and arrange on top of the endive. Arrange the mango and avocado slices on either side of the chicken slices. Sprinkle the diced red pepper over the chicken and drizzle 2 tablespoons of dressing over the avocado and mango. Serve within 30 minutes of preparation.

MANGO CHUTNEY CHICKEN

To serve 6:

6 tablespoons butter

2 tablespoons curry powder

1 teaspoon turmeric

½ teaspoon cumin

½ teaspoon ground ginger

4 tablespoons dry white wine

6 chicken breasts

6 tablespoons mango chutney

3 tablespoons shredded coconut

Preheat the oven to 350°F. Melt the butter in a small pan and add the curry powder, turmeric, cumin and ginger. Cook without browning for 2–3 minutes. Add the wine, stir well to blend and remove from the heat. Place the chicken breasts in an ovenproof dish and baste with the butter and spice mixture. Bake in the oven for 30 minutes. Remove from the oven and spread the mango chutney over the chicken, bake for another 30 minutes basting frequently. Remove the chicken to a serving platter. Pour the pan juices into a small pan and add 2 tablespoons of the shredded coconut. Boil to thicken and reduce the sauce. Pour the sauce over the chicken and sprinkle with the remaining coconut before serving.

CHICKEN SURINAM

To serve 4:

8 oz long-grained rice, cooked

1 small onion, peeled and finely chopped

3 oz butter

1 ripe banana, mashed

1 egg, lightly beaten

1 tablespoon honey

1 teaspoon curry powder

3 tablespoons raisins

1 roasting chicken

1 tablespoon soy sauce

1 tablespoon melted butter

Melt the butter in a saucepan and lightly sauté the onion until transparent. Add the banana and cook together stirring for one minute. Combine together the beaten egg, cooked rice and banana mixture. Add the honey, curry powder and raisins. Mix the ingredients well together and loosely fill the cavity of the chicken. Do not overfill. Truss the bird with string and brush with a mixture of soy sauce and melted butter. Place in a roasting pan in a medium hot oven, 350°F, for 45–60 minutes or until the juices of the bird run clear.

CHILLED CHICKEN PAPRIKA

To serve 6:

3 lb cooked chicken, skinned

½ pint mayonnaise

¼ pint sour cream

1 tablespoon paprika

2 tablespoons tomato purée

½ tablespoon honey

1 teaspoon hot sauce, or to taste

4 large tomatoes, skinned, deseeded and chopped

Cut the chicken into bite-sized pieces. Blend all the remaining ingredients together well and fold in the chicken. Cover and chill for 2–3 hours before serving.

CHICKEN PELAU

A good pelau must be brown – the secret of this lies in the 'browning down' or caramelising of the chicken in a little oil and sugar to give a rich, brown colour.

To serve 6:

½ coconut, meat removed and roughly chopped

Liquid from the coconut

16 oz can pigeon peas

1 medium chilli pepper

½ teaspoon salt

Fresh black pepper

3 tablespoons olive oil

3 tablespoons brown sugar

3 lb chicken breasts

8 oz long-grained rice

½ pint water

For seasoning:
4 green onions, finely chopped

3 cloves garlic, peeled and finely chopped

1 tablespoon chopped chives

1 tablespoon chopped fresh thyme

1 tablespoon chopped fresh parsley

2 celery stalks, scrubbed and finely chopped

4 tablespoons water

Make the seasoning by placing all the seasoning ingredients in a blender with the water and blending until smooth. Make the coconut milk by blending the coconut meat with the liquid in a food processor to form a thick milk. Pour this milk into a saucepan, add the drained pigeon peas and chilli pepper and cook for 15 minutes. Debone the chicken breasts and cut into 2" pieces. In a heavy saucepan heat the oil and sugar together until the sugar caramelises. Add the chicken and coat evenly, cooking for 10–15 minutes, stirring often. Add the pigeon pea mixture, salt and pepper, rice and seasoning to taste and water. Bring to the boil, reduce to a simmer, cover the pan and cook for 20–30 minutes until the rice is cooked. Remove the chilli pepper before serving.

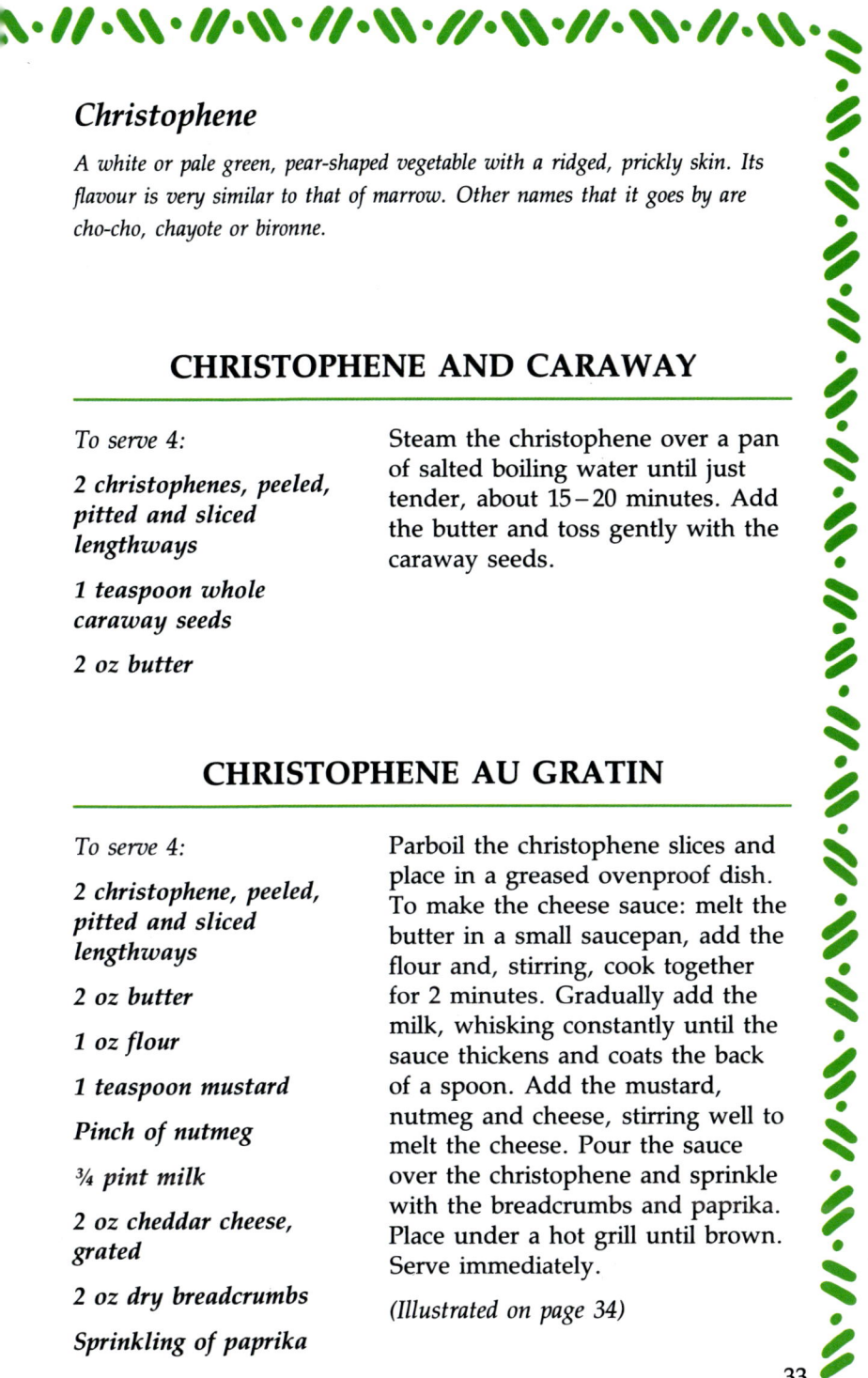

Christophene

A white or pale green, pear-shaped vegetable with a ridged, prickly skin. Its flavour is very similar to that of marrow. Other names that it goes by are cho-cho, chayote or bironne.

CHRISTOPHENE AND CARAWAY

To serve 4:

2 christophenes, peeled, pitted and sliced lengthways

1 teaspoon whole caraway seeds

2 oz butter

Steam the christophene over a pan of salted boiling water until just tender, about 15–20 minutes. Add the butter and toss gently with the caraway seeds.

CHRISTOPHENE AU GRATIN

To serve 4:

2 christophene, peeled, pitted and sliced lengthways

2 oz butter

1 oz flour

1 teaspoon mustard

Pinch of nutmeg

¾ pint milk

2 oz cheddar cheese, grated

2 oz dry breadcrumbs

Sprinkling of paprika

Parboil the christophene slices and place in a greased ovenproof dish. To make the cheese sauce: melt the butter in a small saucepan, add the flour and, stirring, cook together for 2 minutes. Gradually add the milk, whisking constantly until the sauce thickens and coats the back of a spoon. Add the mustard, nutmeg and cheese, stirring well to melt the cheese. Pour the sauce over the christophene and sprinkle with the breadcrumbs and paprika. Place under a hot grill until brown. Serve immediately.

(Illustrated on page 34)

34 *Christophene au gratin*

Cinnamon

The stick form and ground form of this highly aromatic spice is derived from the bark of the Cinnamomum tree. The curly sticks are especially good in hot milky drinks, eggnog, mulled wine, fruit salads and pickles. Ground cinnamon adds a distinctive sweet, spicy flavour sprinkled on biscuits, cakes, toast and in small quantities in some meat dishes.

CLAMS WITH SPICY BREAD STUFFING

To serve 4:

1 pint fresh clams, that have previously been purged

1 tablespoon minced onion

2 cloves garlic, peeled and minced

2 oz fresh breadcrumbs

½ tablespoon minced parsley

1 teaspoon paprika

½ teaspoon hot sauce

Open the clams and using a sharp knife remove the meat from the shell. Mince the meat finely. Combine the clam meat with all other ingredients and blend the mixture well. Place a small amount of the mixture in each half shell to fill and place under a hot grill for 2–3 minutes until the top is brown. Serve immediately.

Cloves

An extremely pungent spice used in the whole, dried berry form or powdered form in curries, stewed fruits, chutneys, pickles, and marmalades. Whole cloves piercing the skin of a baked ham impart a very pleasant hot, sweet and spicy flavour. Remember always to remove whole cloves before serving.

Coconut milk

Coconut milk is extracted from the flesh of a ripe coconut when it is grated and squeezed and is not, as thought, the liquid inside the coconut.

FRESH COCONUT MILK

1 coconut

½ pint water

Crack the nut with a hammer and collect the liquid. Prise the flesh out of the shell, grate into a bowl and add the coconut liquid. Squeeze by hand to extract all the milk or press through a fine sieve. Repeat the process with warm water.

NB: Dessicated coconut can also be used: place 8 oz of dessicated coconut in a blender with 1 pint of hot water. Blend at medium speed for 2–3 minutes and then place in a large bowl and squeeze to extract all the milk or press through a fine sieve.

COCONUT ICECREAM

To serve 6:

2 eggs, separated

4 oz icing sugar

4 tablespoons single cream

1 tablespoon Malibu liqueur

½ pint whipping cream

8 oz fresh shredded coconut

Beat the egg yolks until pale yellow in colour. Beat in the icing sugar and single cream. Cook over a double boiler until the mixture coats the back of a spoon. Remove from the heat and chill. Add the Malibu liqueur. Fold in the whipped cream, stiff whipped egg whites and coconut. Pack well into a mould and still-freeze. Eat within 24 hours.

COCONUT BREAD

To serve 6:

1½ lb plain flour

2 teaspoons baking powder

½ teaspoon salt

8 oz grated coconut

6 oz brown sugar

1 teaspoon vanilla essence

1 egg, beaten

½ pint milk

White granulated sugar for dusting

Sift together the flour, baking powder and salt in a large bowl. Mix in the grated coconut and sugar. Blend together the egg, vanilla and milk and add this mixture gradually to the dry ingredients to form a firm but not sticky dough. Knead for a few minutes and shape into a loaf form. Place in a greased 9" × 4" loaf tin to come three quarters of the way up the tin. Dust the top with the white sugar and bake in a moderately hot oven, 350°F, for approximately 1 hour.

Conch

Pronounced 'conk'. A large mollusc best known for its beautiful conical shell which is coloured delicate shades of pink. To remove the animal from its shell, use a sharp metal instrument to make a hole in the third whorl from the shell apex and cut the adductor muscle which holds the animal in its shell. Ideally, it is best to perform this operation on a sandy beach as the animal produces copious amounts of mucus as it dies. This mucus is very sticky and hard to handle without the addition of sand to the hands to provide some friction. The meat needs to be pounded to tenderise it before cooking and it is imperative to avoid overcooking as this will make the meat tough again. It may be difficult to find fresh conch outside of the Caribbean or Florida but it is available canned. If canned is unavailable then substitute either octopus, squid or abalone.

CONCH FRITTERS

To serve 6:

1 lb conch meat, previously pounded and cut into ¼" pieces

For batter:
2 oz flour

½ tablespoon paprika

1 teaspoon chilli powder

Salt and pepper to taste

1 teaspoon baking powder

2 eggs, beaten

½ pint beer

Sift together all the dry ingredients for the batter. Break the eggs into a small bowl and whisk lightly before adding to a well made in the centre of the seasoned flour. Use a whisk to combine well. Gradually add the beer to make a thick batter and beat well for 3 minutes. Add the diced conch, mixing in well. Leave to stand for at least 1 hour.
After this mix well again. Heat approximately ½" oil in a frying pan and drop scant spoonfuls of the mixture into the hot oil. Turn each fritter once to brown on both sides. Serve immediately. Excellent with a piquant tomato sauce (see page 4).

MARINATED CONCH SALAD

To serve 4:

1 lb conch meat, pounded and cut into 1" slivers

2 tomatoes, peeled, deseeded and finely chopped

1 cucumber, peeled, deseeded and finely chopped

2 tablespoons finely chopped spring onions

6 tablespoons fresh lime juice

2 tablespoons olive oil

Salt and pepper to taste

2 teaspoons hot sauce or to taste

In a large bowl, combine all the ingredients well. Cover and refrigerate for at least 2 hours to marinade the conch. Serve well chilled.

CONCH CHOWDER I

To serve 4:

1 lb conch meat, pounded and finely chopped

1 tablespoon butter

1 medium onion, peeled and chopped

1 green pepper, deseeded and chopped

1 lb potatoes, peeled and cut into ½" cubes

6 oz sweet-corn

2 tomatoes, peeled and roughly chopped

1 tablespoon chopped parsley

Salt and pepper to taste

1 pint fish stock

¼ pint cream

Melt the butter in a heavy saucepan and sauté the onion until transparent. Add the green pepper and potatoes. Cook for approximately 5 minutes, stirring constantly to prevent sticking. Add the flour and cook for 1 minute. Gradually add the stock, stirring to avoid lumps. Simmer gently, stirring until the sauce thickens. Add the sweet-corn, parsley, conch, tomatoes and salt and pepper. Simmer until the potatoes are cooked. Before serving, add the cream and heat through.

Conch chowder

CONCH CHOWDER II

To serve 4:

1 lb conch meat, pounded and finely chopped

1 tablespoon butter

1 medium onion, peeled and chopped

1 green pepper, deseeded and chopped

1 lb carrots, peeled and sliced into rounds

3 oz long grained rice

1 tin peeled plum tomatoes

1 tablespoon basil, roughly chopped

1½ pints fish stock

1 oz flour

Hot sauce to taste

Melt the butter in a heavy saucepan and sauté the onion until transparent. Add the green pepper and carrots. Cook, stirring, for 5 minutes. Add the flour and cook for 1 minute. Add the stock gradually, stirring as the soup thickens. Add the conch, rice, plum tomatoes, basil and hot sauce. Cook until the carrots are tender.

CORNBREAD

To serve 6:

6 oz sifted self-raising flour

2 teaspoons baking powder

2 tablespoons brown sugar

¾ teaspoon salt

10 oz yellow cornmeal

2 eggs

4 tablespoons melted butter

¾ pint milk

Sift together the dry ingredients. Beat together the eggs, melted butter and milk. Beat the liquid ingredients into the dry ingredients with a **few strokes** to form a smooth batter. Pour into a hot, well greased loaf tin, 9″ × 4″ and bake in a hot oven, 425°F for approximately 25–35 minutes. Alternatively, for muffins, drop spoonfuls into well-greased muffin tins and bake at 425°F for 15–20 minutes. Serve hot or cold.

CORN FRITTERS

To serve 4:

12 oz can sweet-corn, drained

1 medium onion, peeled and chopped

½ sweet red pepper, deseeded and finely chopped

1 egg, beaten

¼ pint milk

10 oz flour

1 teaspoon baking powder

1 teaspoon fresh chopped parsley

Salt and pepper to taste

Oil for frying

Hot sauce to taste

In a food processor, blend together the sweet-corn, onion and red pepper. Place this mixture in a bowl and add the egg, sifted flour, baking powder, parsley and salt and pepper. Beat together well. Heat the oil in a frying pan and drop scant spoonfuls of the batter into the hot oil. Turn once so that each side is golden brown. Drain on paper towels. Serve hot with garlic mayonnaise.

CREAM PUNCH

An alcoholic eggnog, popular at Christmas time especially in Trinidad.

To serve 8 (makes 1¾ pints):

1 egg, beaten

Grated rind of 1 lime

½ pint condensed milk

½ pint evaporated milk

¾ pint dark rum

Lots of crushed ice

Angostura bitters

Freshly grated nutmeg to garnish

Place egg, lime rind, milks and rum in a blender and whizz for 30 seconds. Half fill a wine glass with crushed ice and pour the cream punch over. Add a dash of bitters and sprinkling of nutmeg and serve immediately.

CHILLED CUCUMBER SOUP

To serve 4:

2 cucumbers, peeled, deseeded and finely chopped

1 onion, peeled and finely chopped

2 oz butter

½ oz flour

1 pint chicken stock

Salt and pepper to taste

¼ pint single cream

Juice of 2 limes

Fresh mint, to taste

Melt the butter in a saucepan and cook the cucumber and onion together until soft but **not** brown. Add the flour, stirring, and cook for 1 minute. Remove from the heat and add the preheated chicken stock. Season and cook for a further 45 minutes. Blend in a liquidiser until smooth. Add ½ tablespoon finely chopped mint. Cover and chill well. Before serving add the cream and lime juice. Serve very well chilled.

Daiquiri

Rum is ubiquitous throughout the Caribbean, being drunk on any occasion – births, deaths and marriages! It forms the base for the very popular frozen drinks, including diaquiris, where lime juice is the second most important ingredient. Almost any other fruit can be added to make sensational variations.

BANANA DAIQUIRI

To serve 1:

3 tablespoons dark rum

1 tablespoon honey

2 tablespoons lime juice

1 sliced banana

Plenty of crushed ice

Place all ingredients in a liquidiser and blend until smooth. Serve in a frosted tall glass and garnish with glacé cherries, slices of banana and sprigs of mint.

LIME DAIQUIRI

To serve 1:

3 tablespoons white rum

1 tablespoon white sugar syrup

3 tablespoons lime juice

Plenty of crushed ice

Place all ingredients in a liquidiser and blend until smooth. Serve in a frosted tall glass and garnish with wedges of fresh lime.

DOMINICA

This 'banana' republic is the least developed and hence most unspoilt of all the Leeward and Windward Islands. Dominica is a naturalists' paradise with many indigenous species of animals. There are two species of parrot found nowhere else in the world; the Sisserou parrot being displayed on the National flag. The rough, mountainous terrain and lush rainforest make marvellous walks to places with exciting names such as Emerald Falls, The Valley of Desolation, Boiling Lake and Trafalgar Falls. It is the only island in this area with a surviving Carib Indian village tucked far away in the North-east corner of the island, where the artistry of the Indian is still displayed. The capital, Roseau, could be from the turn of the century with its charming wooden houses having the ubiquitous gingerbread and fretwork. Food is plentiful, simple and fresh with little evidence of international or fast food. There are many examples of local fruits and vegetables which are often prepared with the island favourites of fish and mountain chicken (frog). Fresh fish is caught daily around many parts of the island and many of the fishermen converge on Roseau, blowing on conch shells to call the people to the sale.

DUMPLINGS OR SOUP DUMPLINS

These are traditionally made without herbs or spices and can be of any size. These ones are approximately 2" in diameter and can have either cinnamon, mixed spice, parsley or chives added.

To serve 6:

4 oz self-raising flour

2 oz cornmeal

1 teaspoon sugar

Salt to taste

3–4 tablespoons milk

1 oz butter

1 tablespoon chopped parsley

Sift the dry ingredients together into a large bowl. Rub in the butter until the mixture resembles dry breadcrumbs. Mix in the parsley and add the liquid. Mix together to form a dough and then shape to form small balls, slightly flattened. These may now be added to soups or stews as desired.

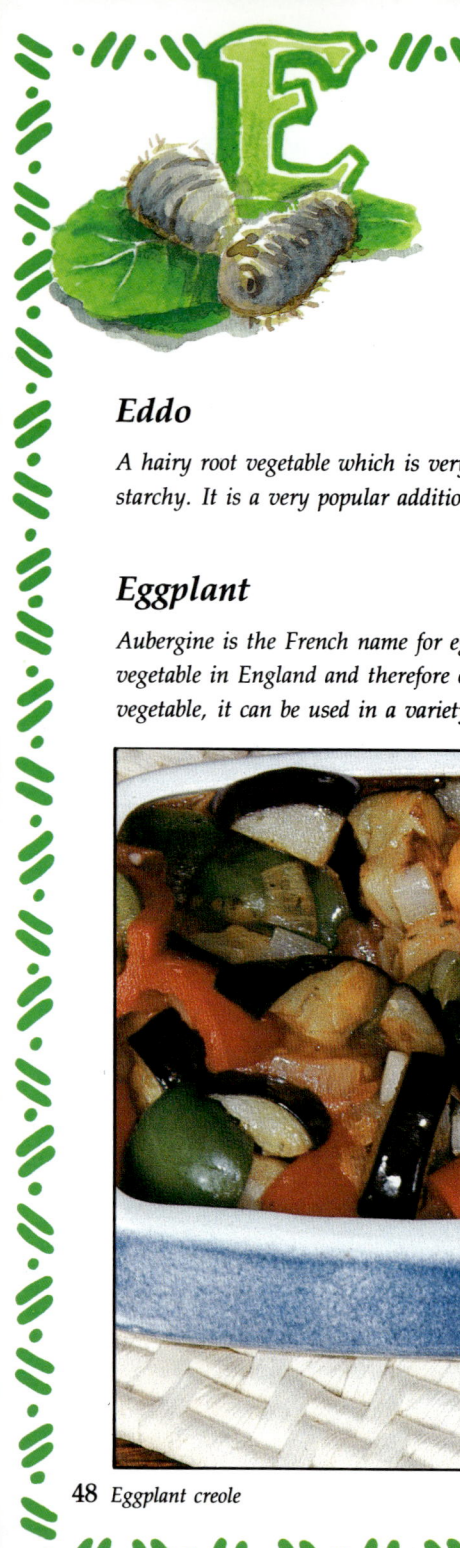

Eddo

A hairy root vegetable which is very similar in taste to the potato but more starchy. It is a very popular addition to soups.

Eggplant

Aubergine is the French name for eggplant; it is also the name given to the vegetable in England and therefore on the British Islands. A very versatile vegetable, it can be used in a variety of hot or cold dishes.

Eggplant creole

EGGPLANT (AUBERGINE) CREOLE

To serve 4:

2 medium eggplants, sliced into ¼" rounds and lightly salted

8 tablespoons olive oil

For creole sauce:
1 large onion, peeled and finely chopped

1 red pepper, deseeded and finely chopped

1 green pepper, deseeded and finely chopped

2 sticks celery, finely chopped

1 teaspoon paprika

½ teaspoon chilli powder

1 tablespoon fresh chopped parsley

4 drops hot sauce or to taste

Salt and pepper to taste

8 oz ripe tomatoes, roughly chopped

Wipe the eggplant slices with a paper towel and lightly fry in the oil. Place in an oiled ovenproof dish. To make the sauce: heat 1 tablespoon olive oil in a heavy saucepan and fry the onion until transparent; add the celery and sauté until soft. Add the green and red pepper and tomatoes and the herbs and spices. Cover and simmer until the sauce has reduced and thickened. Pour over the eggplant and bake in a hot oven, 325°F for 20–25 minutes. Very good with roast meats such as lamb or pork.

SPICY EGGPLANT SALAD

To serve 4:

1¼ lb eggplant, cut into ½" chunks

2 tablespoons white wine vinegar

1 tablespoon red wine vinegar

1 teaspoon paprika

1 teaspoon ground cumin

½ tablespoon tomato purée

1 teaspoon garlic paste

1 teaspoon olive oil

Hot sauce to taste

Place eggplant chunks, white wine vinegar, salt and water to cover in a saucepan. Cover and bring to the boil. Simmer for approximately 5 minutes until soft. Drain well. Mix all the remaining ingredients in a bowl and add the hot eggplant chunks, tossing to coat thoroughly with the dressing. Serve either warm or cold.

ST EUSTATIUS

Locally known as 'Statia', this island has changed hands 22 times, through Dutch, French and the English. It is the poorest of the Windward islands, where traditional economic activities are fishing, farming and trading augmented by an oil storage and refuelling facility. Tourism is the major hope for prosperity. It is historically interesting as in the 1700's, St Eustatius was used as a transhipment point for arms and supplies to George Washington's troops in Boston, New York and Charleston. Geographically it is dominated by a long-extinct volcano, 'The Quill', inside which is lush rainforest where the local sport is to hunt land crabs by moonlight.

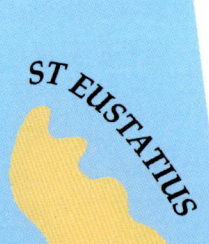

Figs

A smaller, stubbier version of the common banana. Its flavour is also sweeter than the banana. It can be used in the same way.

Fish

The size, colour and variety of Caribbean fish can often be bewildering. Local fishermen use pots on the shallow fringing reef to capture the many varieties of coral fish, which are then usually gutted and cooked whole in a stew or curry, or simply fried. As tasty as these fish can be, they are often rather bony and fiddly and for this reason I have limited my recipes to fish that are larger and firmer of flesh. With the exception of red snapper, these fish are caught on lines, either using a rod or with handlines. The most common types of fish available are kingfish, red snapper, flying fish, dorado, swordfish, tuna, wahoo, grouper and marlin. Kingfish and wahoo are large grey-coloured fish in the same family as tuna but with a lighter coloured flesh and a more delicate flavour. These larger fish are usually cooked in steaks and their firm flesh is excellent for skewering on kebabs or barbecuing. Dorado or dolphin fish is a large, flashy, rainbow-coloured fish with a distinctive bulbous head. Its delicate white flesh has a flavour very similar to mullet. Flying fish is most popular in Barbados where the local fishermen have perfected the technique of filleting these very bony fish. They are a favourite 'street' food, fried and served between slices of bread. With all these fish, if fresh, the very best way to cook them is either filleted or in steaks, grilled with a brushing of butter or oil and served as is or with a garlic or lime butter. Many of the steak fish e.g. swordfish, tuna, wahoo or marlin, are excellent if first marinated in a lime juice and olive oil marinade (which helps prevent drying out when cooking) and then barbecued over a wood fire. Tuna is also very good eaten raw, sliced very thin and dipped in fresh lime juice or dipping sauces such as wasabi or soy sauce. If cooked, tuna should first be brushed lightly with oil or melted butter and then covered in foil as it tends to dry out easily. Sometimes, however, it is nice to have the additional flavours of sauces, e.g. a spicy creole sauce (see 'Eggplant creole') complements the delicate flavour and texture of red snapper. Below is a collection of my favourite recipes for a variety of these Caribbean fish, together with complementary sauces.

WHITE WINE CUCUMBER SAUCE

A lovely pale creamy sauce that is very good with either grouper or red snapper.

1 cucumber, peeled, deseeded and finely chopped

½ oz butter

6 tablespoons white wine

8 tablespoons cream

Black pepper to taste

Lightly salt the cucumber pieces and leave to sweat. Dry with a paper towel. Melt the butter in a saucepan and sauté the cucumber. Add the white wine and pepper and simmer until the wine is reduced to approximately 2 tablespoons. Add the cream and heat through before serving.

GREEN PEPPERCORN SAUCE

Try this tangy sauce with either shark fillets or skate wings.

1 tablespoon green peppercorns

1 tablespoon finely chopped green onion

2 tablespoons white wine

6 tablespoons cream

½ oz butter

Melt the butter in a saucepan and fry the green onion until soft. Add the wine and green peppercorns and simmer for 3 minutes. Add the cream and heat through before serving.

CREAMY LOBSTER SAUCE

Try this delicate pink sauce with either red snapper or dorado.

½ *pint lobster stock (from having boiled lobster) plus the meat from antennae and legs*

1 *teaspoon finely chopped green onion*

¼ *pint cream*

1 *teaspoon tomato purée*

Finely mince any of the leftover lobster meat and add to the stock. Heat the stock and add the green onion. Heat to boiling and simmer to reduce the stock in volume to ⅓ pint. Add the tomato purée and cream and heat through before serving.

Skate wings with pepper sauce

FISH BALLS
with mint dip

To serve 4 (as appetizer):

8 oz fillet of any white fish e.g. snapper, grouper

1 small onion, peeled and finely chopped

3 oz fresh white breadcrumbs

3 – 4 teaspoons freshly chopped parsley

2 teaspoons paprika

2 drops hot sauce

1 egg, beaten

oil for frying

For dip:
6 tablespoons mayonnaise

6 tablespoons sour cream

Salt and pepper to taste

½ tablespoon lime juice

1 tablespoon freshly chopped mint leaves

Place the fish fillet in a liquidiser and blend until smooth. Place the fish, onion, parsley, paprika and hot sauce into a bowl and mix well. Add the beaten egg to bind the mixture together. Form the mixture into walnut-sized pieces and fry in a little oil until golden brown. Serve hot with the dip. To make the dip: combine all the ingredients and chill.

SHARK FILLETS
with pepper sauce

To serve 4:

4 6 oz shark fillets

Juice of 2 limes

2 oz butter

1 clove garlic, minced

1 small onion, peeled and finely chopped

1 red pepper, deseeded and thinly sliced

1 green pepper, deseeded and thinly sliced

1 yellow pepper, deseeded and thinly sliced

1 teaspoon hot sauce

2 tomatoes, peeled, deseeded and finely chopped

1 tablespoon finely chopped fresh parsley

Salt and pepper to taste

Cover the shark fillets with lime juice in a bowl and leave for 30 minutes. In a heavy frying pan melt 1 oz of butter and gently sauté the onions and peppers. Add the hot sauce and tomatoes and simmer for 10 minutes. Add the parsley and salt and pepper to taste. Melt the remaining butter in a small pan and add the lime juice marinade. Grill the shark fillets under a hot grill for approximately 5 minutes each side, basting with the butter/lime marinade mix. To serve, top the shark fillets with the pepper sauce.

WEST INDIAN FISH SOUP

To serve 8:

3 tablespoons olive oil

4 cloves garlic, peeled and minced

2 onions, peeled and finely chopped

2 carrots, peeled and sliced

1 sweet potato, peeled and finely diced

1 can peeled plum tomatoes

Juice of 1 lime

1 green pepper, deseeded and chopped

1–2 teaspoons hot sauce or to taste

1 teaspoon basil

1 teaspoon parsley

1 bay leaf

Salt and pepper to taste

1½ pints fish stock

½ lb of any white fish (reserving the heads) cut into ½" cubes

¼ pint dry white wine

½ lb raw shrimp

¼ lb clams

Heat the oil in a large saucepan and sauté the onion, garlic, carrot and sweet potato until they are golden brown. Add the stock and peeled tomatoes, herbs and salt and pepper and simmer gently until the vegetables are nearly cooked. Add the white wine, fish (and heads), green pepper, hot sauce and lime juice. Stir well, lower the heat and simmer for 20–30 minutes until the fish is cooked. Add the shrimps and clams and simmer for a further 5 minutes until the shrimp are cooked. Serve with or without the fish heads, accompanied by a green salad and garlic bread.

FISH CURRY
with eggplant and tomato

To serve 6:

2 tablespoons oil

¼ teaspoon mustard seed

1 large onion, peeled and finely chopped

Thin slice of fresh ginger, peeled and grated

1 clove garlic, sliced

10 oz eggplant, peeled, cut into quarters and soaked in water

Pinch of turmeric

¼ teaspoon cumin

¼ teaspoon aniseed

Pinch of nutmeg

Salt and pepper to taste

1 fresh green chilli, sliced

3 curry leaves

2 tablespoons curry powder

¾ pint water

1 teaspoon vinegar

2 ripe tomatoes, cut into quarters

1½ lb firm fish, e.g. kingfish or similar

2 tablespoons coconut milk

1 tablespoon lime juice

Heat the oil in a large saucepan, add the mustard seed and fry for a couple of seconds. Add the onions and fry until golden brown. Reduce the heat and add the ginger, garlic, eggplant, turmeric, cumin, aniseed, nutmeg, salt and pepper to taste, chilli, curry powder and leaves and water. Stir and then add the vinegar and boil for 5 minutes, covered. Add the fish, tomatoes and coconut milk. Simmer gently for 15 minutes or until the fish is cooked. Add the lime juice, bring to the boil and remove from the heat. Serve immediately with rice and a green salad.

FISH WITH FRESH CHILLIS AND TAMARIND

To serve 4:

½ teaspoon chilli powder

2½ tablespoons curry powder

Salt and pepper

1 tablespoon tamarind paste

Pinch of turmeric

½ pint water

3 tablespoons oil

1 large onion, peeled and thinly sliced

Thin slice of ginger, peeled and grated

6 fresh green chillis, halved

2 lb whole fish, e.g. kingfish, Spanish mackerel, cut into ½" steaks

1 teaspoon vinegar

2 tablespoons evaporated milk

1 teaspoon peanut oil

In a bowl mix the chilli powder, curry powder, salt, pepper, tamarind paste, turmeric and water to form a watery paste. Cover and put aside. Heat the oil in a saucepan, add the onion and fry until golden brown. Add the ginger and chillies, fry for 2 seconds only and then add the spice paste. Fry this for 5 minutes, stirring continuously. Reduce the heat to low and add the fish and vinegar. Stir well, cover and simmer until the fish is cooked. Add the evaporated milk and peanut oil, mix well and bring to the boil, remove from the heat and serve with white rice.

FRUIT SORBET

To serve 2:

Juice from 2 limes

½ banana

1 mango, peeled and pitted

1 coconut

2 oz caster sugar

1 egg white

Break the coconut over a bowl and collect the liquid, reserve the flesh for later use. Mix the banana, mango flesh, lime juice, caster sugar and coconut water in a liquidiser and blend until smooth. Pour into a bowl. Whip the egg white until stiff and fold gently into the fruit mixture. Freeze in a shallow container. When it is almost frozen, whizz again in the blender and return to the freezer until solid. Remove from the freezer approximately 15 minutes before serving.

Genips

A round, bright green fruit of approximately 1" diameter. The shell can be popped open between two fingers to reveal a large, gelatinous seed which when sucked tastes like lime.

Ginger

The pungent, peppery flavoured rhizome (commonly referred to as root) of the Zingiber *plant. Whole fresh or green ginger should have a smooth skin and be a uniform buff colour. The time of harvest is very important or the texture will be fibrous and have a bitter after-taste. The whole root is best stored in a plastic bag in the refrigerator. Ginger can also be purchased in a powdered, less pungent form.*

GINGER BEER

Traditionally a Christmas drink, it is now commonly drunk at any time as it is very sweet and refreshing.

To make 1 gallon:

1 lb green root ginger

1–1½ lb white granulated sugar

1 gallon water

Dried orange peel

6 cloves

1 teaspoon cinnamon

Peel and cut the ginger into small pieces and place in a saucepan with the water. Bring to the boil and boil for 30 minutes. Add the sugar, stir well to dissolve, cover and allow to cool. Add the cloves, orange peel and cinnamon. Pour into a basin and leave covered for 2 days at room temperature. Strain and refrigerate.

GINGER BREAD

To serve 6:

8 tablespoons molasses

8 oz sugar

4 oz butter

8 tablespoons hot water

10 oz plain flour

2 teaspoons baking powder

½ teaspoon salt

1 teaspoon nutmeg

2 teaspoons freshly grated ginger

1 egg, beaten

Mix the molasses, sugar and butter together in a saucepan and heat gently. Pour in the hot water, mix well and set aside. Sift together the flour, baking powder, salt and nutmeg, then add the grated ginger and egg. Combine the molasses mixture with the flour mixture and pour the resultant batter into a shallow, greased tin lined with greased paper. Bake at 325°F for 1 hour.

Ginger bread

Another beautiful, verdant island located at the end of the chain of Leeward and Windward isles in the south of the Caribbean Sea. There are mountains, sandy beaches, lush rainforests, waterfalls and hot springs in abundance. Grenada is also known as the 'Spice Island' since the dense rainforests are full of exotic spice trees. One third of the world's nutmeg is grown here as well as large quantities of mace, cloves and cinnamon. There is also a wild profusion of cocoa, bananas, sugar cane, mangoes, breadfruit, avocadoes, oranges and limes. Grenada has a large manufacturing industry from agricultural produce such as chocolate, sugar, rum, jams, coconut oil, honey and lime juice; also a large brewery and rice mill. An added attraction of the island is its very colourful market which is situated in the capital, St Georges. From the sea, this town is seen as a colourful horseshoe-shaped bay of pastel tinted houses which might have been transplanted from some small Cornish town but was, in fact, established by the French in 1705.

By far the most exotic and memorable food on the island is served at a local restaurant called 'Mammas', found on the outskirts of St Georges. The menu is changed each day according to what fresh produce is available and all meals are served family style. A typical evening meal might consist of an astonishing array of West Indian cuisine: curried goat, chicken stew, opossum, snake and armadillo stews, okra creole, a variety of rice and bean dishes, all brought to the table simultaneously. Other popular foods are souse (a sauce made from pigs' feet), pepperpot and pumpkin pie. Nutmeg features in many of the dishes, nutmeg jelly for breakfast and ground nutmeg on top of rum punch. The term 'grog' for rum is thought to have originated from Grenada, being the first letters of 'Georgius Rex Old Grenada' which was stamped on the casks of rum sent back to England.

THE GRENADINES

A group of small islands, islets and rocks situated between St Vincent and Grenada. The main ones are Bequia, Mustique, Union, Canouan, Mayreau, Petit St Vincent and the Tobago Cays being governed by St Vincent; with Carriacou and Petite Martinique being governed by Grenada. Bequia has a large white and mixed race population. Remnants of the Nova Scotians came to whale here in the last century. The remains of the small whaling industry may still be seen on a small offshore islet and until fairly recently was used to launch the sailing whalers. Petit St Vincent (PSV) is a complete island resort; Mustique is an island 'getaway' for the rich and famous; Tobago Cays is a group of tiny islets and sand bars with spectacular diving and snorkling; on Carriacou the local carpenters still build the local 50–60' trading vessels using adzes and hand saws.

GINGER AND PAPAYA COCKTAIL

To serve 4:

1 large ripe papaya, peeled, deseeded and cut into long slices

Juice and zest of 2 limes

4 pieces of stem ginger and 1 tablespoon of the syrup

Arrange the slices of papaya on four individual plates. Chop the ginger into small pieces and sprinkle onto the papaya. Combine the lime juice and stem ginger syrup and drizzle over. Garnish with the lime zest.

GUADELOUPE

One of the two major French islands in the region, it is a Department of France and as such enjoys the prosperity of France as well as the excellent wines and food. Many of the restaurants have an interesting mixture of French and Creole cuisine.

Guava

A small, golf-ball sized fruit with a pale yellow, wrinkled skin covering a pale pink, succulent flesh which in turn covers a seed-laden soft pulp. The fruit has a sweet, spicy smell and the pulp is used to make jams, jellies, drinks and desserts.

GUAVA CHEESE

Guavas

Sugar

Chop the guavas coarsely and press through a sieve. To each ½ pint of the resultant juice, add 8 oz sugar. Place this mixture in a heavy saucepan and boil over a medium heat, stirring constantly until the mixture thickens and leaves the side of the saucepan. Pour into a shallow tin and when cold and nearly set, cut into squares. Dust with icing sugar and store in sterilised jars.

HEARTS OF PALM SALAD

This is supposedly the most expensive salad in the world, as it is made from the central core of the Royal Palm tree. If it is not available fresh, then the canned variety will substitute.

To serve 4:

8 oz heart of palm

1 red pepper, deseeded and finely sliced

1 yellow pepper, deseeded and finely sliced

4 tablespoons olive oil

4 tablespoons white wine vinegar

Black pepper to taste

Slice the hearts of palm into ½" rounds. Toss all the ingredients together gently and chill well before serving.

Hot peppers

The Scotch Bonnet pepper is probably the hottest pepper available. Hot sauce, made predominantly from these peppers, is a very popular condiment in the West Indies. It is normally used sparingly in soups, stews and fried fish although many people shake it straight onto their food!

HOT SAUCE

To make 1½ pints:

1 green papaya, peeled, deseeded and roughly chopped

5 Scotch Bonnet peppers (or green chillis), deseeded and chopped

1 yellow sweet pepper, chopped

1 red sweet pepper, chopped

1 onion, peeled and chopped

4 tomatoes, chopped

4 cloves garlic, peeled and minced

4 tablespoons lime juice

Zest of 1 lime

¾ pint malt vinegar

½ teaspoon salt

1 tablespoon Worcester sauce

4 tablespoons mustard

Place the papaya, peppers, onions, tomatoes, garlic, lime zest and juice in a liquidiser and blend until nearly smooth. Transfer to a saucepan and stir in the vinegar, salt, Worcester sauce and mustard. Simmer for 20 minutes, stirring occasionally. Bottle the sauce in sterilised jars.

J

Jamaica is the third largest island in the Caribbean, forming the Greater Antilles along with Cuba and Hispaniola. It is perhaps the most scenically beautiful of the islands, having 200 miles of white sandy beaches, 120 rivers and streams and lush mountainous vegetation – all this packed into only 146 miles stretching east to west and approximately 40 miles north to south.

JAMAICA

Of the 2.5 million inhabitants, 95 per cent are of African or Afro-European descent – 'Out of many, one people' is the National motto. The island is also home to the Rastafarians with their distinctive reggae music. The island has a long tradition of exotic, flavourful cooking, the most notable being ackee and saltfish (the national dish), peas 'n' rice (made with kidney beans, not peas) and bammy cakes – a delicious flat cake made with cassava flour. Meat patties are a Jamaican staple snack – pastry filled with spicy ground beef and breadcrumbs.

Agriculture and tourism are the main props of the national economy. In particular sugarcane (the by-products of which are rum and molasses) bananas, pimento and coffee. Mineral mining also brings in a large part of the income.

ST JOHN — The most unspoilt of the US Virgin Islands, due mainly to the creation of a National Park on approximately ⅓ of the island by the Rockefeller family.

Jerk

This method of cooking is probably South American in origin. Jerk pork or pork jerky is the most popular recipe used today. To prepare, the blood is collected from a freshly slaughtered pig and mixed together with hot peppers, pimentoes, nutmeg, cinnamon, green onions and salt and pepper to form a thick paste. The pig is scraped of all its hair and the entrails removed. The paste is then rubbed all over the body and it is slowly roasted over a fire of green pimento wood. The meat turns almost black owing to a combination of the blood, seasoning and pimento wood.

JERKED PORK CHOPS

To serve 6–8:

4 lb pork chops

2 oz pimento berries

6 green onions, finely chopped

2–3 hot peppers

4 fresh bay leaves

Salt and pepper to taste

Wash and dry the pork chops. Heat the pimento berries in a small frying pan, stirring them for approximately 5 minutes. Place them in a mortar and pound them until they are powdery. Add the green onions, hot pepper, bay leaves and salt and pepper. Pound these until a thick paste has formed and rub this over the meat. Leave the meat for at least an hour or better overnight in the refrigerator. The meat may be grilled under a hot flame or over charcoal made from pimento wood or regular charcoal. Turn the meat after about 15–20 minutes.

Jerked pork chops

BARBECUED KIDNEY BEANS

To serve 4:

8 oz tin red kidney beans

4 tablespoons tomato ketchup

2 tablespoons malt vinegar

1 teaspoon mustard

½ teaspoon garlic paste

1 tablespoon Worcester sauce

1 tablespoon brown sugar

Hot sauce to taste

Salt and pepper to taste

Beat together the ketchup, vinegar, mustard, garlic, Worcester sauce, sugar, hot sauce and condiments. Mix the drained beans into this mixture and place in an oven-proof dish. Bake at 425°F for approximately 45 minutes or until the beans just start to blacken on top.

ST KITTS

Sixty eight square miles comprising three groups of volcanic peaks split by deep ravines. A low-lying peninsula contains saltponds and spectacular beaches. Like its close neighbour Nevis, St Kitts has a fine collection of historical stone buildings. The local spirit CSR (Cane Spirit Rothschild), is produced by Baron de Rothschild and is drunk neat with ice, with water or with Ting—the local grapefruit soft drink.

SPICY LAMB STEW

In the West Indies this dish is usually made with goat meat.

To serve 6:

2 lb stewing lamb, fat trimmed and cut into 1" cubes

2 tablespooons olive oil

1 large onion, peeled and roughly chopped

1 green pepper, deseeded and roughly chopped

2 large carrots, peeled and sliced

8 oz cooked chick peas

¾ pint stock

1 oz flour

2 – 3 tablespoons curry powder

2 tablespoons grated coconut

Black pepper

⅓ pint sour cream

Heat the oil in a large saucepan and add the onion, pepper and carrots. Cook for 5 minutes until softened. Add the curry powder and flour, stir and cook for 2 minutes. Add the lamb and sauté until browned. Add the stock gradually until the sauce is made. Add the grated coconut and chick peas and simmer gently until the lamb is tender. Add the black pepper and sour cream and heat through before serving.

ROAST LEG OF LAMB
with garlic and guava glaze

To serve 8:

5 lb leg of lamb

4 cloves garlic, peeled and cut into slivers

¼ pint guava jelly

1 teaspoon ground rosemary

Salt and pepper

Preheat the oven to 450°F. Insert the garlic slivers under the skin of the leg of lamb using a sharp pointed knife. Brush generously with the guava jelly and sprinkle on the rosemary and salt and pepper to taste. Place the meat fat-side up on a roasting rack, and place in the hot oven for 10 minutes. Reduce the oven to 350°F and cook uncovered for 30 minutes per lb for well done or 25 minutes per lb for slightly rare. Use the pan juices to make the gravy and add more guava jelly if desired.

Lime juice

Pre-Colombian Amerindians of the islands liked to mix the green part of crab meat with lime juice, making a sauce called tamaulin, which was eaten with cassava bread. This is the earliest evidence of lime juice being used as a seasoning and a marinade. This habit was adopted by all newcomers to the islands as a method of marinading, as the taste of fresh fish and meat was considered to be 'too strong or fresh'.

LIME SQUASH

To serve 1:

Juice of 3 limes

Sugar to taste

Soda water

Stir the sugar into the lime juice until it has dissolved. Add soda water to fill the glass. Serve with lots of ice.

LIME DELIGHT

To serve 4:

6 oz condensed milk

Whites of 2 eggs

Juice and zest of 4 limes

Mix together the milk, lime juice and zest. Whisk the egg whites until stiff and fold gently into the milk mixture. Chill well before serving.

LOBSTER AVOCADO SALAD

To serve 4:

2 avocados

¾ lb lobster meat, finely shredded

4 green onions, finely chopped

1 clove garlic, minced

2 drops hot sauce

1 tablespoon fresh chopped parsley

Juice of 1 lime

1 tablespoon olive oil

Red leaved lettuce

Halve each avocado, remove the stone and scrape out the flesh. Mash the flesh in a bowl until smooth and add the green onions, garlic, hot sauce, parsley, lime juice, shredded lobster meat and olive oil. Mix well and chill for at least one hour. Serve on a bed of red lettuce.

(Illustrated on page 74)

ST LUCIA

Another spectacularly beautiful island with the twin Piton peaks in the south. These forest-clad extinct volcanic plugs rise sheer out of the sea to a height of 2600'. Sadly, this marvellous area of natural beauty has been developed into a resort. Marigot Bay on the south-west corner of the island is probably one of the most picturesque harbours in this group of islands.

Lobster avocado salad

LOBSTER WITH GARLIC OR LIME BUTTER

To serve 2:

2 1½ lb fresh lobsters, cooked

4 oz butter

4 cloves garlic, minced, or juice of 3 limes

Salt and pepper to taste

Using a meat cleaver and hammer, split each lobster tail in half lengthways and place the meat (still in its shell) meat-side up on a grill pan. Melt the butter and allow to simmer for 2–3 minutes. Leave to stand and ladle off the surface residue. Add either garlic or lime juice. Brush the lobster with the butter and place under a hot grill for 10 minutes until browned. Brush with butter during grilling to prevent the meat drying out. Serve immediately.

LOBSTER THERMIDOR

To serve 2:

2 1½ lb lobsters, cooked, tail meat removed and diced

1 oz butter

1 oz flour

¼ pint fish stock or lobster water from cooking

1 small onion, peeled and finely chopped

1 small green pepper, deseeded and finely chopped

½ teaspoon French mustard

1 tablespoon brandy

½ pint double cream

4 oz parmesan cheese

Melt the butter in a heavy saucepan. Add the onion, green pepper and lobster meat and sauté gently for 2 minutes. Add the flour and cook, stirring continuously for 1 minute. Add the stock gradually and stir as the sauce begins to thicken. Add the mustard and brandy and three quarters of the cheese. Finally add the cream and stir well together. Refill the lobster shells with this mixture, sprinkle with the remaining cheese and place under a hot grill until just browned.

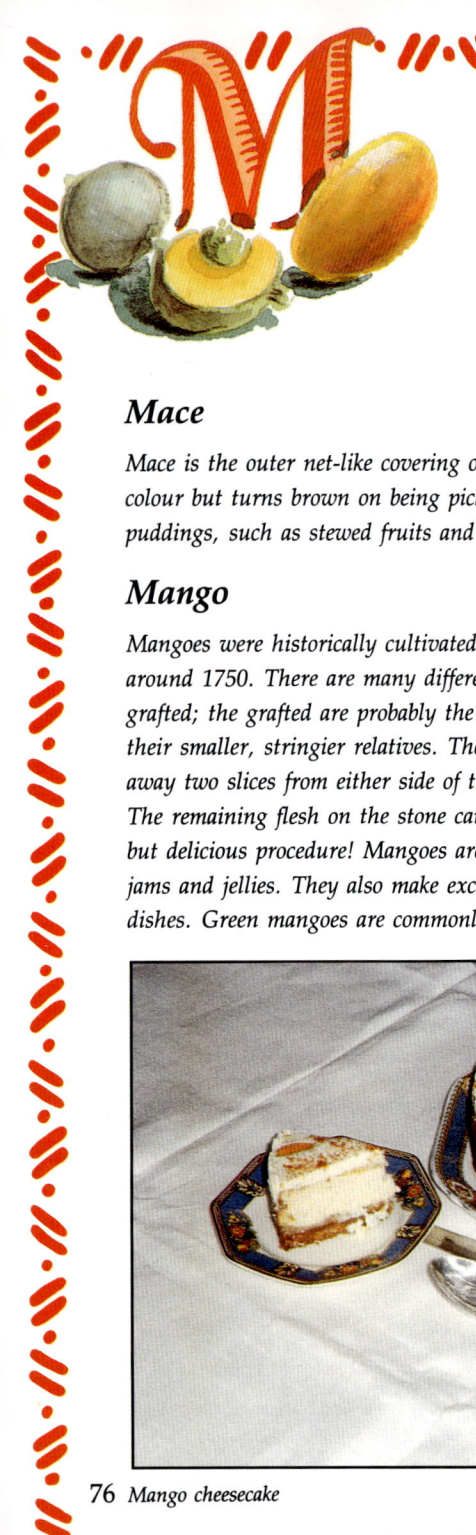

Mace

Mace is the outer net-like covering of the nutmeg pod. It is bright red in colour but turns brown on being picked and sun-dried. It is used for flavouring puddings, such as stewed fruits and drinks.

Mango

Mangoes were historically cultivated in India and first appeared in Barbados around 1750. There are many different varieties from wild, cultivated to grafted; the grafted are probably the best as they are large and juicy unlike their smaller, stringier relatives. The best way to eat a whole mango is to cut away two slices from either side of the stone. Eat the flesh from the two slices. The remaining flesh on the stone can be sucked off too – an extremely messy but delicious procedure! Mangoes are commonly used to make desserts, drinks, jams and jellies. They also make excellent sauces for chicken, pork or lamb dishes. Green mangoes are commonly used in chutneys and curries.

Mango cheesecake

MANGO CHEESECAKE

To serve 6:

8 oz digestive biscuits, crushed into crumbs

1 oz brown sugar

3 oz butter, melted

2 eggs, well beaten

1 lb soft cream cheese

4 oz white sugar

1 teaspoon lemon juice

½ teaspoon salt

4 tablespoons mango pulp

1 teaspoon ground cinnamon

¼ pint sour cream

2 tablespoons brown sugar

½ teaspoon vanilla essence

Mango slices to decorate

To make the biscuit base, mix the biscuit crumbs with the melted butter and 1 oz of brown sugar. Press firmly into an 8" spring form pan and chill well. Preheat the oven to 375°F. Beat together the eggs, cream cheese, white sugar, lemon juice and salt. Fold in the mango pulp, pour onto the biscuit base and bake for 20 minutes. Remove from the oven, dust with cinnamon and allow to cool. Turn the oven up to 425°F. Mix together the sour cream, sugar and vanilla, pour over the cake and bake for 5 minutes. Allow to cool and then arrange the mango slices decoratively on top. Refrigerate for at least 6 hours before serving.

ST MARTIN

Two cultures in one island, Dutch Sint Maarten pulsing with duty-free shops (selling every kind of electrical item), casinos and nightclubs; French St Martin with fashion houses and excellent restaurants. There are no border formalities, just a modest monument erected in 1948 commemorating the division of the island three centuries earlier.

MANGO CHUTNEY

To make 1½ pints:

12 mangoes, slightly under-ripe

2 oz fresh ginger, peeled and roughly chopped

3 cloves garlic, peeled and minced

4 oz shelled tamarinds

1 hot pepper or hot sauce to taste

8 oz raisins

8 oz brown sugar

¾ pint malt vinegar

Peel the mangoes, remove the flesh and roughly chop into chunks. Scrape the pulp from the tamarind and chop the hot pepper finely, discarding the seeds. Place the mango chunks, ginger, garlic, tamarind and hot pepper in a large saucepan with the raisins, sugar and vinegar. Bring to the boil and then simmer until the mixture thickens. Stir from time to time to prevent sticking. Pour into sterilised jars.

MANGO FOOL

To serve 2:

1 ripe mango, peeled and flesh removed

3 teaspoons orange liqueur

1 – 2 tablespoons natural yoghurt

1 small orange, peeled and sliced

Put the mango flesh and orange liqueur into a liquidiser and blend to a smooth purée. Fold in the yoghurt. Reserve a few slices of orange for decoration and roughly chop the rest, dividing between individual serving dishes. Pour the mango purée on top. Chill and decorate with the reserved orange slices before serving.

MANGO ICECREAM

To serve 4–6:

8 eggs, separated

8 oz caster sugar

½ pint double cream

1 lb fresh mango pulp

½ teaspoon lemon juice

Set the freezer control to maximum or quick freeze before starting. Whisk the egg whites until stiff, add the caster sugar and whisk for a further 2–3 minutes. In another bowl, whisk the cream until just firm. Beat the egg yolks and fold into the egg whites. Fold in the cream and mango pulp and add the lemon juice. Pour the mixture into a large tub and place in the freezer. Whip after 1–2 hours or when just firm to the touch. Return to the freezer and freeze until hard. Remove from the freezer approximately 15 minutes before serving.

MANGO SHERBET

To serve 4–6:

½ pint water

8 oz sugar

3 large mangoes, peeled and flesh cut into 1" chunks

1 tablespoon fresh lemon juice

1 egg white

Place the water and sugar in a small, heavy saucepan and heat, stirring, until the sugar dissolves and the mixture boils. Boil uncovered for 1 minute then remove from the heat. Cool the syrup to room temperature, then refrigerate, covered, until cold (about an hour). Purée the mango pulp with the lemon juice in a liquidiser until smooth. Add the egg white and whizz to blend. Transfer the mixture to a large bowl and whisk in the syrup. Freeze tightly covered for several hours or longer if possible to allow the flavours to mellow. Remove from the freezer approximately 15 minutes before serving.

Market scenes

The market scene of today has not changed much from the days of the great plantations. The main market area is usually located in the capital, often housed in an open-sided colonial building with rusty Victorian ironwork. Inside are row upon row of wooden benches selling all manner of fruits, vegetables, herbs, spices and pepper sauces. The shade affords some coolness although most of the women prefer to display their wares, haphazardly arranged on oil cloths, in the blazing sun. Sitting on tiny wooden stools, often with a large umbrella to shade them, these voluminous women laugh and shout to one another while tempting you to sample their produce. Fruits and vegetables are sold by number or weight and often you cannot buy one type without the inclusion of another, even if you do not want it! For example, to buy 3 lb of potatoes you may have to include 1 lb of carrots, particularly if one of these is in short supply. The display is exotic, colourful and pungent; huge prickly pineapples, papayas in various stages of ripeness from bright green to orange, juicy mangoes, scarlet petals of sorrel, red sweet potatoes, hairy brown yams, thick knobbly fingers of ginger, bundles of sweet-smelling lemon grass and of course, everywhere, huge stems of green bananas and piles of jelly nuts – the green coconuts with their sweet water. It is an experience that will assault the senses – the cacophony of gossipy tongues, the fresh pungency of food and its multicoloured garishness.

MARTINIQUE

Another Department of France. Its capital, Fort-de-France, has a distinct suburban flavour and, after the relative backwardness of the other islands, the fast pace and chic atmosphere is rather a shock to the system. There is a delightful blend of French, African and Indian influences in the cooking – well-seasoned spicy blood sausage, Ti-Boudin; blaff (conch, snapper or sea urchin cooked in lime, white wine and onions); accras (spicy fish fritters originating from Africa); poulet-au-coco (chicken with onions, hot peppers and coconut). Main dishes are accompanied by either white rice, yams, breadfruit or sweet potatoes with red beans or lentils.

SPICY MEATBALLS
with garlic and dill dip

To serve 4:

1 lb minced beef

4 oz breadcrumbs

Salt and pepper to taste

1 medium onion, peeled and finely chopped

1 tablespoon freshly chopped parsley

½ tablespoon mustard

1 egg, beaten

For dip:
¼ pint mayonnaise

¼ pint sour cream

1 tablespoon freshly chopped dill

4 cloves garlic, peeled and minced

Mix together the beef, breadcrumbs, seasoning, onion, parsley, mustard and beaten egg, binding together well. Pinch off walnut sized pieces, shape into rounds and place on a greased baking tray. Cook for 20–25 minutes in a hot oven, 425°F. Combine all the ingredients for the dip thoroughly and chill well before serving with the meatballs, which may be served hot or cold.

(Illustrated on page 82)

MONTSERRAT

The pear-shaped 'Emerald Isle'; volcanic in origin with an active fumarole and hot mineral springs. Montserrat was established as an Irish Catholic colony in the 1600's, where Catholic refugees fled to escape persecution. A strong Irish influence is still apparent: on arrival at the airport your passport is stamped with an Irish Shamrock; the National dish, Goat Water, is based on the Irish stew recipe. Since 1783 the island has been under British rule. Today, the island has become a popular retreat for recording artists in the music industry.

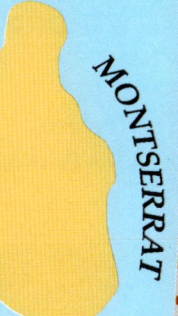

Spicy meatballs with garlic and dill dip

SPICY MEAT PATTIES

To serve 4:

1 lb short crust pastry

1 lb minced beef

2 carrots, peeled and finely chopped

1 medium onion, peeled and finely chopped

Salt and pepper to taste

½ teaspoon hot sauce

1 egg, beaten

Combine all the ingredients together for the meat filling. Roll out the pastry and divide into four squares. Divide up the meat mixture into four and place one quarter on each of the pastry squares. Fold one corner over to its diagonal opposite. Brush each with beaten egg and bake in a hot oven, 375°F, for 30 minutes. Can be served hot or cold.

NEVIS

A 'charming' island, full of interesting history and many examples of old plantation houses which have been restored and converted into guest houses and restaurants. Admiral Lord Horatio Nelson met and married Fanny Nesbit here. It was also home to Alexander Hamilton, who helped draft the Constitution of the United States. The spa baths, which are still standing, were much visited by wealthy Europeans in the last century. The former capital, Jamestown, was drowned by a tidal wave in 1680 but can still be visited by snorklers.

Nutmeg

Nutmeg is the inner kernel of the fruit of the tree, Myristica officinalis. *It is an aromatic spice with a nutty, spicy flavour and has even been known to be addictive. It is best kept whole, being grated as the need arises so that the aroma is preserved. It is very good on spinach, white meats, eggnog, puddings, cakes and, of course, rum punch.*

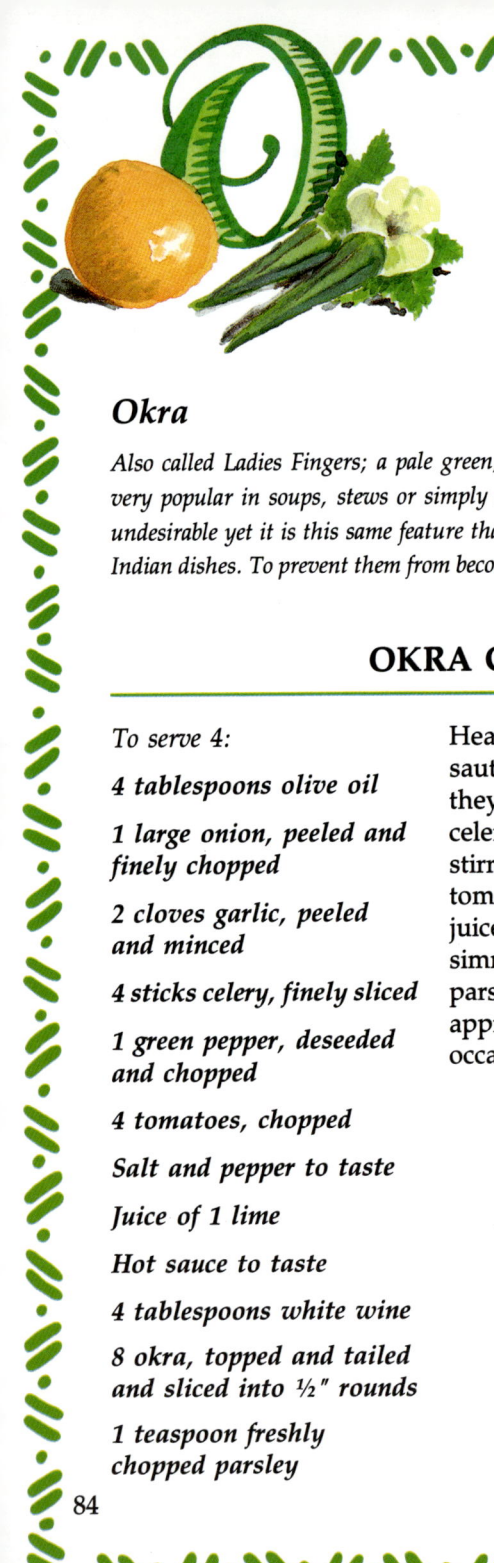

Okra

Also called Ladies Fingers; a pale green, hexagonal shaped vegetable which is very popular in soups, stews or simply sautéed. Some find their stickiness undesirable yet it is this same feature that enhances many of the traditional West Indian dishes. To prevent them from becoming too sticky, wash and dry before use.

OKRA CREOLE

To serve 4:

4 tablespoons olive oil

1 large onion, peeled and finely chopped

2 cloves garlic, peeled and minced

4 sticks celery, finely sliced

1 green pepper, deseeded and chopped

4 tomatoes, chopped

Salt and pepper to taste

Juice of 1 lime

Hot sauce to taste

4 tablespoons white wine

8 okra, topped and tailed and sliced into ½" rounds

1 teaspoon freshly chopped parsley

Heat the oil in a large pan and sauté the onion and garlic until they are golden brown. Add the celery and green pepper. Cook, stirring, for 2 minutes. Add the tomatoes, salt and pepper, lime juice and white wine. Heat to simmering and add the okra and parsley. Mix well and cook for approximately 30 minutes, stirring occasionally.

Papaya

Also called paw-paw and considered to be both a fruit and a vegetable. It is often used as a natural meat tenderiser. It can be used green in soups and stews but is far better if left to ripen to a golden orange colour and eaten fresh. The thin, outer skin covers the orange, sweet-scented 'melt-in-the-mouth' flesh which in turn hides a mass of black, wrinkled seeds embedded in a thick, clear, gelatinous film. Papaya is wonderful eaten raw with just a squeeze of lime and is equally delicious in fruit salads or fresh milk shakes.

PAPAYA MOUSSE

To serve 8:

1 pint papaya pulp, approximately 2 large ripe fruit

6 oz white icing sugar

1½ teaspoons gelatin

2 tablespoons cold water

4 tablespoons boiling water

2 tablespoons lime juice

½ pint whipping cream

Add the icing sugar to the papaya pulp in a large bowl and mix together well. In a smaller bowl, soak the gelatin in the cold water until thick and then add the boiling water to dissolve it. Add this gelatin mixture to the papaya, mix well and allow to cool. Fold the lime juice and the whipped cream into the mixture. Cover and chill well before serving.

Passion fruit

This spherical, sometimes tear-shaped fruit was named after the suffering of Christ. It has a delicate combination of flavours – lemon, pineapple and guava.

PASSION FRUIT FOOL

To serve 4:

¾ *pint passion fruit pulp*

Icing sugar to taste, approximately 1 tablespoon

½ *pint whipping cream*

1 tablespoon kirsch

Add the sugar to the fruit pulp in a large bowl and leave for 10 minutes. Fold in the whipped cream and kirsch, pour into individual dishes and chill well before serving.

PEANUT AND BANANA PUNCH

To serve 2:

1 pint milk

5 tablespoons condensed milk

½ banana

3 tablespoons smooth peanut butter

¼ teaspoon cinnamon

¼ teaspoon vanilla essence

Large handful crushed ice

Place all the ingredients in a liquidiser and blend until smooth. Serve immediately.

Pepperpot

An Arawak dish similar to a very spicy stew. In Arawak times the pepperpot was said to be generations old, as each day it was replenished with more vegetables and meat. The principal ingredients are small game and callaloo, the whole dish being flavoured with lots of hot peppers.

PINA COLADA

To serve 1:

2 oz dark rum

4 oz pineapple juice

1 oz coco lopez – cream of coconut

Squeeze of fresh lime

Plenty of crushed ice

Place all the ingredients in a liquidiser and blend well until smooth. Serve immediately in a tall glass with cherries and a slice of pineapple.

Pineapple

There are many different varieties of pineapple grown in the Caribbean. By far the tastiest and most succulent is the Antiguan Black Pineapple which has spiky leaves. The French islands produce a larger but less sweet variety that has smooth leaves. To test a pineapple for ripeness, pull a leaf from the centre of the leaf crown. If it comes away easily then the fruit is ripe.

PINEAPPLE FLAMBÉ

To serve 4:

1 fresh pineapple, peeled and sliced into ½" rounds

2 oz butter

2 oz brown sugar

3 tablespoons dark rum

Melt the butter in a large frying pan and add the sugar. Stir until it has melted and then add the pineapple slices, turning to coat with the butter. Cook for 2–3 minutes and then add the rum and ignite when hot. Flame off the alcohol and serve immediately.

SCALLOPED PINEAPPLE AND CORN

To serve 4:

1 fresh pineapple, peeled and flesh finely chopped

8 oz fresh or frozen sweet-corn

2 oz brown sugar

2 oz flour

4 oz mild cheddar, grated

Butter

8 tablespoons vegetable stock

Place the stock in a saucepan and bring to the boil over a low heat. Add the flour, whisking constantly then add the sugar, whisking until thick. Place the pineapple, corn and cheese in a buttered ovenproof dish and pour the sauce over. Dot with butter and bake for 30 minutes at 325°F.

Plantains

A larger member of the banana family which must be cooked. Often used in soups, stews or desserts; green plantains are usually boiled while the riper, sweeter plantains are sliced and fried and are very good as an accompaniment to fried fish.

CARIBBEAN ROAST PORK

To serve 10:

6 lb leg of pork

10 cloves garlic, peeled and sliced

4 tablespoons Worcester sauce

½ tablespoon salt

½ tablespoon black pepper

½ tablespoon ground oregano

½ tablespoon thyme

½ tablespoon Dijon mustard

3 bay leaves

2 tablespoons clear honey

2 oz butter

½ pint strong coffee

½ pint milk

¼ pint fresh orange juice

Salt and pepper

Wash the leg of pork and pat dry. Make incisions in the skin using a pointed knife and insert the garlic slivers. Set the leg in a large roasting pan. Combine the Worcester sauce, pepper, oregano, thyme, mustard and bay leaves to form a thick paste and rub it all over the pork leg. Cover with plastic wrap and place in the refrigerator for 2 days, basting 3–4 times. Preheat the oven to 350°F. Turn the pork, skin-side up in the pan, brush the surface with 1 tablespoon of honey and dot with butter. Roast for 15 minutes and then add half the coffee and half the milk. Roast for a further 30 minutes. Turn the pork over, brush the surface with remaining honey and add the rest of the coffee and milk. Roast for 30 minutes, basting. Add the orange juice and salt and pepper and continue roasting until the juices run yellow. Stand for 15 minutes before carving and use the juices to make the gravy.

CREOLE PRAWNS
served in a potato straw basket

To serve 4:

3 potatoes

Oil for deep frying

1 tablespoon olive oil

1 lb peeled prawns

1 medium onion, peeled and finely chopped

2 cloves garlic, peeled and finely chopped

1 red pepper, deseeded and roughly chopped

1 green pepper, deseeded and roughly chopped

1 stick celery, thinly sliced

3 okra, topped and tailed and sliced into rounds

4 tomatoes, peeled and roughly chopped

1 tablespoon tomato purée

¼ pint fish stock

1 teaspoon basil

1 teaspoon chopped parsley

1 teaspoon paprika

½ teaspoon chilli powder

1 tablespoon flour

Hot sauce to taste

To make potato straw baskets:
Peel and roughly grate the potatoes. Line the inside of a metal sieve with a layer of grated potato and place a second sieve inside the first to hold the potato in place. Lower into a hot deep fat fryer and fry until golden brown. Make four baskets and keep warm until the prawn creole is completed.

To prepare prawn creole:
Heat the olive oil in a heavy pan and add the onion and garlic, cooking until transparent. Add the paprika, chilli powder and flour and cook, stirring, for 1 minute. Add the stock, tomato purée and hot sauce to taste. Add the peppers, okra and celery and cook for 2–3 minutes before adding the tomatoes and prawns. Cook until the prawns are opaque.

To serve, fill each basket with the creole sauce and sprinkle with the chopped parsley.

Creole prawns served in a potato straw basket

Pumpkin and ginger soufflé with a caramelised net

Pumpkin

The flesh of the Caribbean pumpkin is bright orange with a sweet flavour and firm texture. The skin is variegated green and white. This vegetable makes an excellent soup.

PUMPKIN SOUP

To serve 6:

1½ lbs fresh pumpkin, peeled, deseeded and cut into ½" cubes

2 oz butter

1 large onion, peeled and chopped

2 cloves garlic, peeled and minced

2 potatoes, peeled and chopped

2 carrots, peeled and sliced

1 pint chicken stock

1 teaspoon turmeric

¼ teaspoon ground ginger

¼ teaspoon ground cinnamon

½ pint cream

Chopped parsley

Melt the butter in a heavy pan and add the garlic and onion. Sauté gently until the onion is transparent. Add all the spices and cook for 1 minute. Add the pumpkin, potatoes and carrots, stir well and add the stock. Cover and simmer until the vegetables are tender. Place in a liquidiser and blend until smooth. Add the cream and heat through before serving. Garnish with the chopped parsley.

PUMPKIN AND GINGER SOUFFLÉ
with a caramelised net

To serve 8:

6 large eggs, separated

8 oz fresh puréed pumpkin, cooked

2 oz stem ginger, finely minced

1 teaspoon ground cinnamon

½ oz gelatin

3 tablespoons water

4 oz granulated white sugar

¼ pint water

Mix together the pumpkin purée, stem ginger and cinnamon in a large bowl. Put the yolks and whites of the separated eggs into separate bowls. Beat the egg yolks until creamy and pale and add them to the pumpkin mixture. Dissolve the gelatin in the 3 tablespoons of water and then stir this into the pumpkin and yolk mixture. Leave until just beginning to thicken but not setting. Whisk the egg whites until they stand in soft peaks and then gently fold into the pumpkin mixture. Pour into a 1 pint soufflé dish with a collar of oiled greaseproof paper around the top. Place in the refrigerator until set and then remove the greaseproof paper. Make the caramelised net by boiling the granulated sugar with the ¼ pint of water until pale golden in colour. Leave to cool slightly and then drizzle onto greaseproof paper to form a network of caramel strands. When this has cooled and hardened, place it on top of the soufflé.

(Illustrated on page 91)

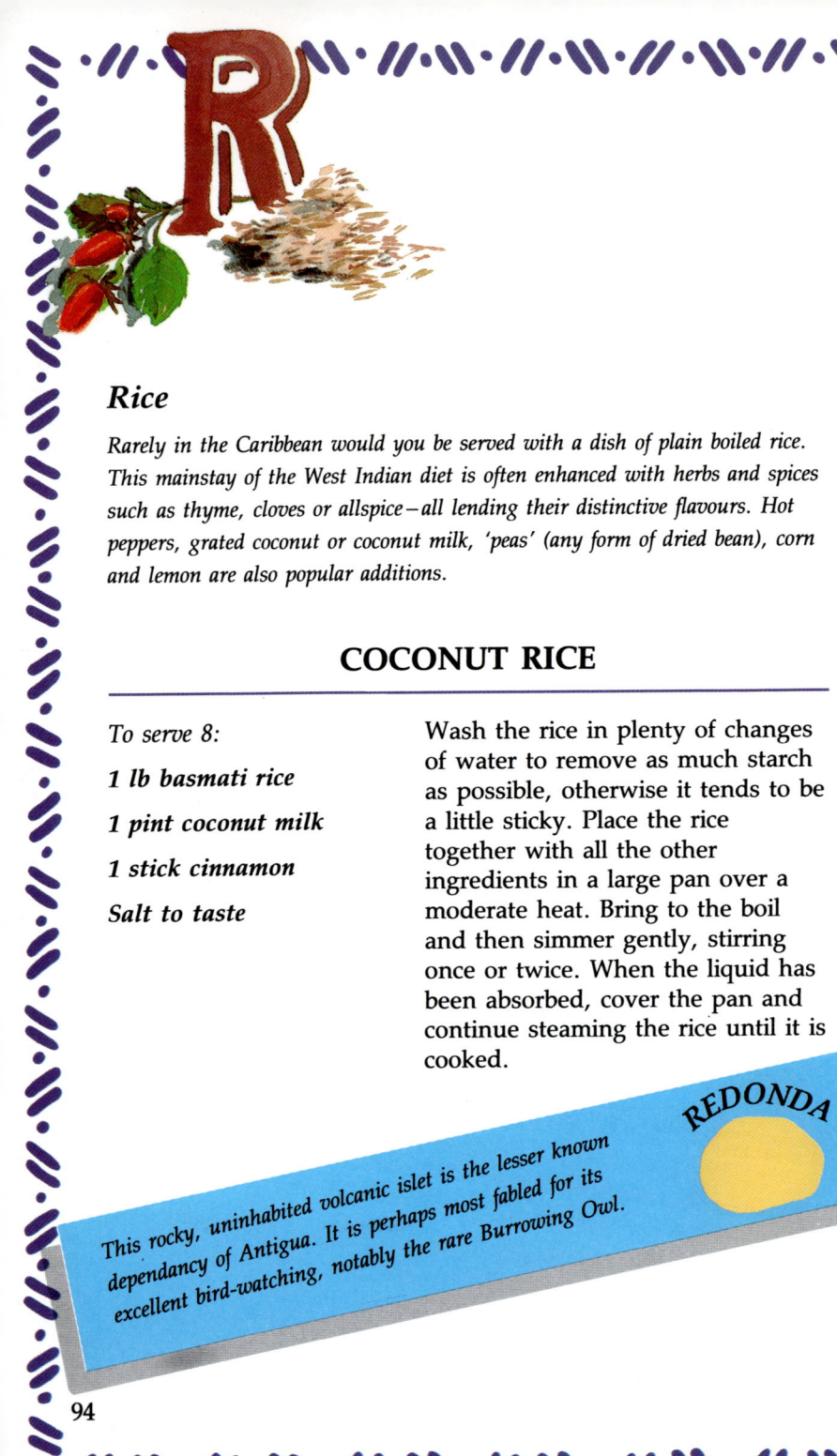

Rice

Rarely in the Caribbean would you be served with a dish of plain boiled rice. This mainstay of the West Indian diet is often enhanced with herbs and spices such as thyme, cloves or allspice—all lending their distinctive flavours. Hot peppers, grated coconut or coconut milk, 'peas' (any form of dried bean), corn and lemon are also popular additions.

COCONUT RICE

To serve 8:

1 lb basmati rice

1 pint coconut milk

1 stick cinnamon

Salt to taste

Wash the rice in plenty of changes of water to remove as much starch as possible, otherwise it tends to be a little sticky. Place the rice together with all the other ingredients in a large pan over a moderate heat. Bring to the boil and then simmer gently, stirring once or twice. When the liquid has been absorbed, cover the pan and continue steaming the rice until it is cooked.

REDONDA

This rocky, uninhabited volcanic islet is the lesser known dependancy of Antigua. It is perhaps most fabled for its excellent bird-watching, notably the rare Burrowing Owl.

LEMON AND GARLIC RICE

To serve 4:

6 oz long-grained rice

1 oz butter

2 cloves garlic, peeled and crushed

Sprinkle of turmeric

4 tablespoons lemon juice

½ pint water

Hot sauce to taste

Salt to taste

Chopped fresh chives to garnish

Melt the butter in a large pan and fry the garlic until it is golden brown. Add the rice, turmeric, lemon juice, water, hot sauce and salt. Bring to the boil, cover and simmer for 10 minutes. Remove the lid and cover loosely with tin foil, replace the lid and steam until the rice is cooked. Serve garnished with chives.

RICE AND PEAS

To serve 8:

8 oz blackened or pigeon peas, cooked

½ teaspoon thyme

2 oz creamed coconut

1 medium onion, peeled and finely chopped

2 cloves garlic, peeled and chopped

1 stick cinnamon

1 lb long-grained rice

1 tablespoon butter

Place all the ingredients in a large pot and simmer for 30 minutes. Steam-cook the rice by covering with foil when all the water has been absorbed. Traditionally served with lots of hot sauce.

ROTI BREAD

Introduced to the Caribbean in the Nineteenth century by the East Indians; it is a flat, unleavened bread used to wrap around curried chicken, beef, goat or conch and potatoes.

To serve 4:

8 oz self-raising flour

2 teaspoons baking powder

½ teaspoon salt

½ teaspoon sugar

1 tablespoon lard

4 tablespoons water

Sift together the flour, baking powder, salt and sugar in a large bowl. Rub in the lard and add enough water to make a soft dough. Cover and set aside for 1 hour. Divide the dough into four portions and roll out each portion into a 5" circle approximately ¼" thick. Heat an ungreased pan until hot enough to make a drop of water sizzle. Place each roti bread on the pan for approximately 2 minutes until the bottom starts to brown. Remove from the pan and place the desired filling in the centre of the round. Fold the edges like a parcel to seal well.

RUM PUNCH

To serve 1:

1 part sour – lime juice

2 parts sweet – sugar syrup or Grenadine syrup

3 parts strong – rum

4 parts weak – water, or a mixture of orange and grapefruit juice

Mix all the ingredients well and serve in a tall glass over plenty of crushed ice. Decorate with a slice of pineapple or lime and freshly grated nutmeg.

Chicken roti

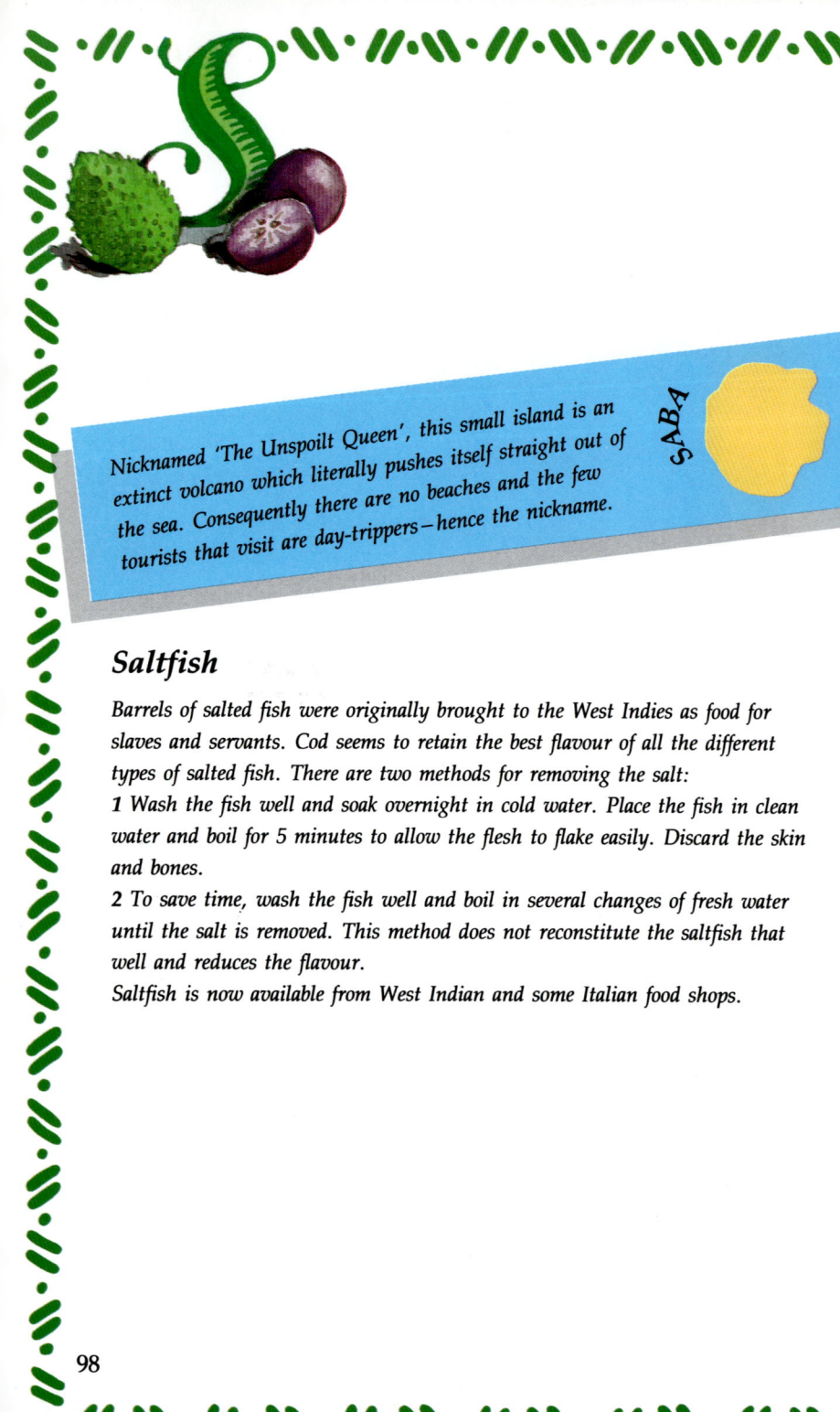

Nicknamed 'The Unspoilt Queen', this small island is an extinct volcano which literally pushes itself straight out of the sea. Consequently there are no beaches and the few tourists that visit are day-trippers – hence the nickname.

SABA

Saltfish

Barrels of salted fish were originally brought to the West Indies as food for slaves and servants. Cod seems to retain the best flavour of all the different types of salted fish. There are two methods for removing the salt:

1 Wash the fish well and soak overnight in cold water. Place the fish in clean water and boil for 5 minutes to allow the flesh to flake easily. Discard the skin and bones.

2 To save time, wash the fish well and boil in several changes of fresh water until the salt is removed. This method does not reconstitute the saltfish that well and reduces the flavour.

Saltfish is now available from West Indian and some Italian food shops.

SALTFISH AND ACKEE

To serve 4:

8 oz saltcod

2 oz butter

3 tablespoons olive oil

1 clove garlic, peeled and minced

4 rashers streaky bacon

6 spring/green onions, finely chopped

1 small onion, peeled and finely chopped

½ teaspoon thyme, chopped

½ teaspoon parsley, chopped

1 Scotch Bonnet pepper, deseeded and finely chopped

1 yellow pepper, deseeded and finely chopped

1 red pepper, deseeded and finely chopped

3 tomatoes, finely chopped

12 oz can ackees, drained

Salt and pepper to taste

Parsley to garnish

Heat the oil and butter in a shallow frying pan, add the bacon and fry until crisp. Remove from the pan, drain excess oil. Fry the onions, thyme, parsley and peppers together for 5 minutes. Add the tomatoes and cook for a further 5 minutes. Prepare the saltcod as above and add the flaked flesh to the onion and tomato mixture. Add the ackees and bacon and cook for 2–3 minutes until heated through. Garnish with parsley before serving.

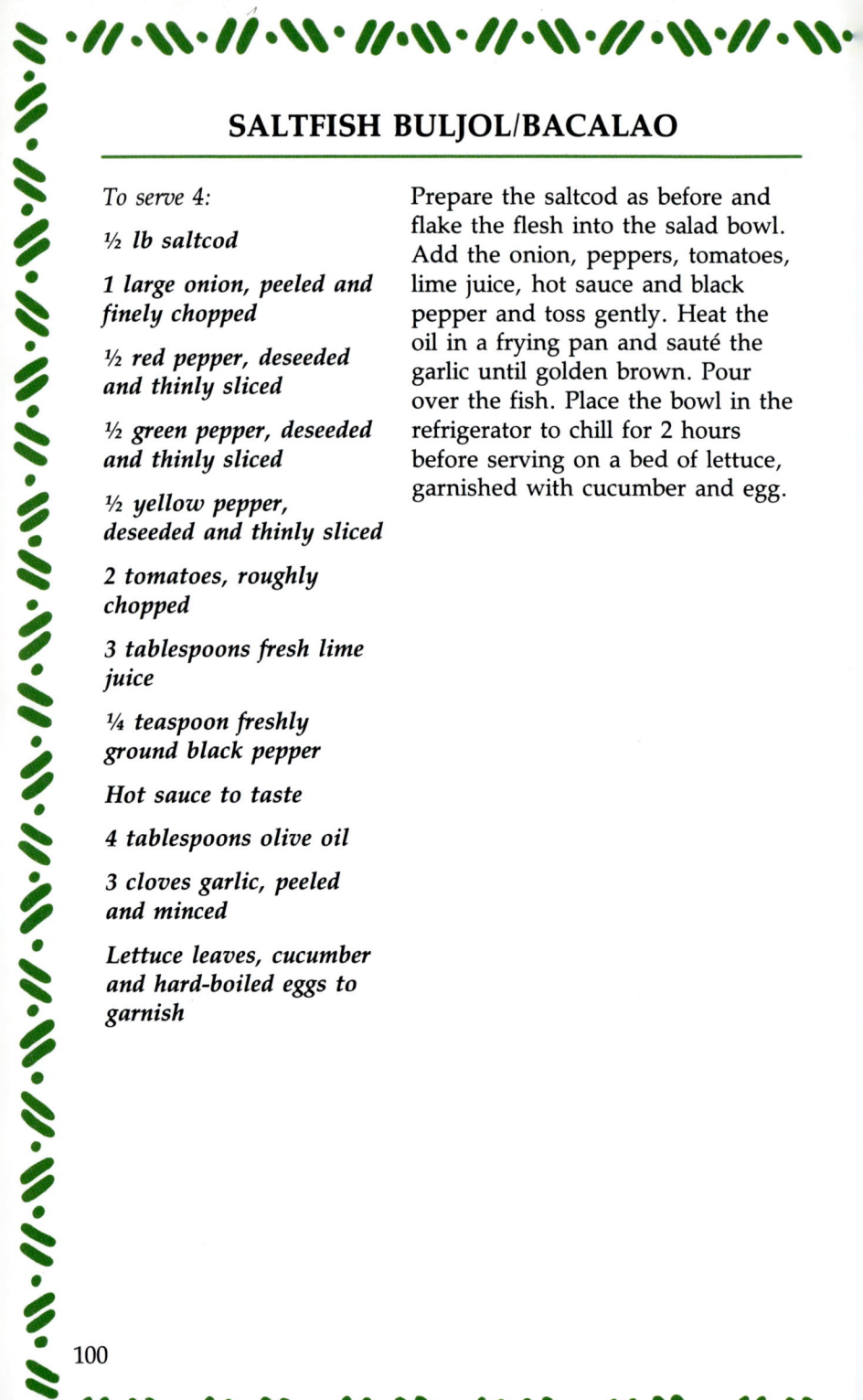

SALTFISH BULJOL/BACALAO

To serve 4:

½ lb saltcod

1 large onion, peeled and finely chopped

½ red pepper, deseeded and thinly sliced

½ green pepper, deseeded and thinly sliced

½ yellow pepper, deseeded and thinly sliced

2 tomatoes, roughly chopped

3 tablespoons fresh lime juice

¼ teaspoon freshly ground black pepper

Hot sauce to taste

4 tablespoons olive oil

3 cloves garlic, peeled and minced

Lettuce leaves, cucumber and hard-boiled eggs to garnish

Prepare the saltcod as before and flake the flesh into the salad bowl. Add the onion, peppers, tomatoes, lime juice, hot sauce and black pepper and toss gently. Heat the oil in a frying pan and sauté the garlic until golden brown. Pour over the fish. Place the bowl in the refrigerator to chill for 2 hours before serving on a bed of lettuce, garnished with cucumber and egg.

SEAFOOD GUMBO

To serve 6:

1 lb King prawns or shrimp

2 pints water

2 tablespoons butter

2 tablespoons flour

4–6 oz okra, sliced

1 large onion, peeled and roughly chopped

1 stalk celery, roughly chopped

1 green pepper, deseeded and roughly chopped

2 cloves garlic, peeled and minced

4 large tomatoes, chopped

1 sprig thyme

1 tablespoon chopped parsley

2 bay leaves

Hot sauce to taste

1 tablespoon Worcester cause

4 oz pumpkin, peeled, deseeded and finely chopped

½ lb fresh crab meat

1 lb fresh tuna, kingfish or any firm fish, cut into small chunks

Shell the prawns or shrimp and devein. Make a stock using the shells and water, cooking for approximately 1 hour. Strain off the stock and reserve. Melt the butter in a large saucepan, add the okra and sauté until less sticky. Add the onion, celery, pepper and garlic. Cook, stirring, for a few minutes. Add the flour and continue to cook for 1 minute. Add the stock, blending well to prevent lumps. Add the tomatoes and all other ingredients and simmer gently until the pumpkin and fish are cooked. Serve with green salad and cornbread (page 42).

CHILLED SHRIMP BISQUE

To serve 6:

6 oz cream of celery soup concentrate

12 oz tomato or V8 juice

8 oz peeled, deveined, cooked shrimp, roughly chopped

Juice of 2 limes

Hot sauce to taste

Salt and pepper

¼ pint cream

Finely chopped parsley and lime zest, for garnish

Whisk together all the ingredients except the cream and garnish in a large bowl. Chill well for several hours. Before serving, add the cream and mix well. Serve in chilled bowls garnished with the parsley and lime zest.

CURRIED SHRIMP SOUP

To serve 4:

2 tablespoons ground almonds

2 tablespoons dessicated coconut

¼ pint boiling water

2 oz butter

1 onion, peeled and finely minced

2 sticks celery, finely chopped

1 oz plain flour

1 tablespoon curry powder

¼ teaspoon ground cumin

1 pint fish stock

2 teaspoons lime juice

Salt, pepper and hot sauce to taste

½ pint milk

6 oz shrimps, peeled and deveined

4 tablespoons cream

Place the almonds and coconut in a bowl, cover with the boiling water, stir and leave to cool. Drain off the resultant liquor and reserve. Melt the butter in a large pan and sauté the onion and celery gently until just soft. Stir in the flour, curry powder and cumin and cook, stirring, for 1 minute. Add the stock and coconut liquor, blending well, and bring to the boil. Add the lime juice, salt and pepper and hot sauce. Cover and simmer for 20 minutes. Stir in the milk and shrimp, reserving four for the garnish. Simmer for 5 minutes or until the shrimp are cooked. Allow to cool and then chill. Before serving in chilled bowls add the cream and then garnish with the reserved shrimp.

SHRIMP SAUTÉED IN GARLIC BUTTER

To serve 4:

1 lb fresh jumbo shrimp, peeled and deveined

3 oz butter

6 cloves garlic, peeled and minced

Black pepper to taste

Fresh finely chopped chives, to garnish

Rinse the shrimp well under cold running water and pat dry. Melt the butter in a large frying pan, add the garlic and fry for 1 minute. Add the shrimp and, stirring constantly, cook them for approximately 5 minutes or until just opaque. Do not overcook as they will tend to become rubbery. Sprinkle on the black pepper, stir once and serve immediately sprinkled with chives. Delicious served with coconut rice (page 94).

Shrimp in lime-ginger sauce

SHRIMP WITH COCONUT IN GARLIC BUTTER

To serve 4:

1 lb fresh jumbo shrimp, peeled and deveined

2 oz butter

2 cloves garlic, peeled and minced

1 tablespoon dessicated coconut

1 tablespoon coconut milk

Freshly chopped parsley for garnish

Rinse the shrimp well under cold running water and pat dry. Melt the butter in a large frying pan, add the garlic and fry for 1 minute. Add the shrimp and dessicated coconut. Cook, stirring constantly until the shrimp are just opaque. Add the coconut milk and cook for a further 2 minutes. Serve immediately sprinkled with parsley.

SHRIMP IN LIME-GINGER SAUCE

To serve 4:

1 lb fresh jumbo shrimp, peeled and deveined

2 oz butter

1 tablespoon finely grated fresh ginger

1 tablespoon finely grated lime peel

Juice of 1 lime

Freshly chopped parsley for garnish

Rinse the shrimp well under cold running water and pat dry. Melt the butter in a large frying pan, add the ginger and sauté for 1 minute. Add the shrimp and cook, stirring constantly until just opaque. Add the lime peel and juice and cook for 2 minutes. Serve immediately sprinkled with parsley.

Sorrel

A bright red fruit with a tart flavour. The fleshy sepals are used to make a traditional Caribbean Christmas drink.

SORREL DRINK AND RUM

To make 1 gallon:

1½ lb fresh sorrel, pitted

2 oz grated green ginger

1 gallon water

Sugar to taste

Rum to taste, preferably a dark rum, either Cavalier or Mount Gay

Place the sorrel and ginger in a large container, add the boiling water and stir well. Cover and leave for 24 hours. Strain through a fine sieve or muslin. Add the sugar and rum and serve in a tall glass over lots of crushed ice.

Soursop

A dark green, pear-shaped fruit covered with rough spiky nodules. It can grow to varying sizes. The creamy white pulp, embedded with shiny black pips, has a spicy, sweet smell with a slightly tart flavour. It is popular as an ingredient in milkshakes and icecream.

SOURSOP CREAM

To serve 4:

1 ripe soursop, peeled and deseeded

½ pint single cream

Grated nutmeg, to taste

Place the soursop in a liquidiser and blend until smooth. Stir in the cream and nutmeg and chill well before serving.

Sweet potato

This very versatile vegetable came originally from tropical South America. It is often mistaken for yam. The flesh can vary in colour from white to pink to orange to red-brown, and can be cooked in a variety of ways, in either sweet or savoury dishes.

CANDIED SWEET POTATOES

To serve 4:

2 lb sweet potatoes

3 oz butter

½ tablespoon ground cinnamon

¼ tablespoon ground ginger

1 tablespoon brown sugar

Peel the potatoes and slice into ½" slices. Parboil, drain and arrange in a shallow, buttered, ovenproof dish. Dot with the butter, sprinkle on the sugar and spices and bake at 325°F for 30–35 minutes until the butter is bubbling and just turning brown.

(Illustrated on page 108)

CREAM OF SWEET POTATO SOUP

To serve 6:

4 oz butter

2 leeks, white part only, thinly sliced

2 pints chicken stock

4 tablespoons white wine

4 large sweet potatoes, peeled and chopped

Zest and juice of 1 lime

½ teaspoon ground turmeric

¼ teaspoon ground cumin

¼ pint milk

¼ pint cream

Salt and pepper to taste

Melt the butter in a large pan and sauté the leeks until transparent. Add the turmeric, cumin and sweet potatoes and sauté for 1–2 minutes. Add the stock and wine and bring to the boil. Reduce the heat and simmer for approximately 15–20 minutes or until the potatoes are tender. Add the lime juice and zest, salt and pepper. Place the soup in a liquidiser and blend until smooth. Return to the pan and add the milk and the cream. Can be served hot or cold.

Candied sweet potatoes

SWEET POTATO PUDDING

To serve 6:

5 tablespoons brown sugar

2 eggs, beaten

Pinch of salt

2 drops vanilla essence

4 oz butter

3 tablespoons custard powder

4 oz coconut cream, mixed with ⅓ pint of water

¼ pint evaporated milk

1 lb sweet potatoes, boiled and mashed

Mix together the sugar, beaten eggs, salt, vanilla essence and 2 oz of butter in a large bowl. Cream well together. Add the coconut cream, water, evaporated milk and mashed sweet potatoes and beat together well to form a smooth batter. Pour the batter into a well greased ovenproof dish and dot the top with the remaining butter. Bake at 350°F until the pudding sets. Cut into squares and serve warm or cold.

Tamarind

The Tamarind tree originated from the East Indies. The shiny brown pods, which can grow up to 6" in length, contain dark seeds covered in a brown flesh. The spicy pulp has a sharp date/apricot flavour and is used to flavour stews and curries as well as forming the base of many sauces such as Worcester, pepper and brown sauce.

Tropical fresh fruit salad

TROPICAL FRESH FRUIT SALAD

To serve 6:

½ pineapple, peeled and cut into 1" chunks

2 mangoes, peeled, pitted and cut into slices

½ honeydew melon, peeled, deseeded and cut into chunks

1 avocado, peeled, pitted, and cut into slices

1 papaya, peeled, deseeded and cut into slices

2 bananas, peeled and cut into slices

For syrup:
¼ pint water

¼ pint orange juice

Juice of 1 lime

1 teaspoon ground ginger

1 teaspoon cinnamon

Arrange the fruit decoratively in a glass bowl in the order in which they appear in the list of ingredients.

Heat all the syrup ingredients together in a saucepan and boil for 5 minutes or until a thick syrup forms. Allow to cool and pour over the fruit. Chill well before serving.

(Illustrated on page 109)

ST THOMAS

'Paradise Island of the USA' proclaims the car licence plates. St Thomas is the largest of the US Virgin Islands, so named by Columbus in 1493 after St Ursula and her 1000 virgin warriors. There is a plethora of high rise hotels, crowded towns, fast cars and duty-free shopping, hence it is a very popular island with cruise ships.

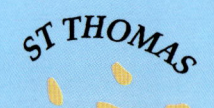

Turmeric

The golden colour of this spice lends the underlying colour to curry powder. Consequently, it is often used as a food colouring in small quantities, especially in rice dishes, where it can replace the more expensive saffron. It has a hot, acidic flavour that should be used with caution in curries.

TORTOLA

This is the main island of the British Virgin Islands, which is slowly but surely catching up with the development of the US Virgin Islands.

TRINIDAD & TOBAGO

Southernmost of the islands in the Caribbean chain, the two islands which constitute the Republic of Trinidad and Tobago lie only 7 miles from the South American mainland. Unlike the other Caribbean islands they are not the product of ancient volcanoes but a gradual breech between South America and a small mountainous region on her North-east coast. Trinidad is a 'paradise of interracial harmony', containing probably the most heterogeneous people on Earth. Indians and Africans make up about 80 per cent of the population. Immigrants from the Far and Middle East arrived as traders. The European element comes mainly from the Spanish, French and British—all at one time rulers of the island. Because of the rich variety of cultures, Trinidadians may one day eat a hot Indian curry, the next day, a Creole pelau, the next, French black pudding, saltfish buljol, Chinese char-sue pork and Spanish pastelles. The most popular 'fast-food' is roti.

In vivid contrast, Tobago has unspoilt beaches—deserted save for fishermen or groups of local children, bumpy roads and tiny hamlets where tourists are an interesting anomaly rather than an oppressive necessity! Culinary notables are curried crab and dumplings, fish broth, cassava bread and some excellent homemade wines—pineapple, breadfruit, mango, cashew and banana.

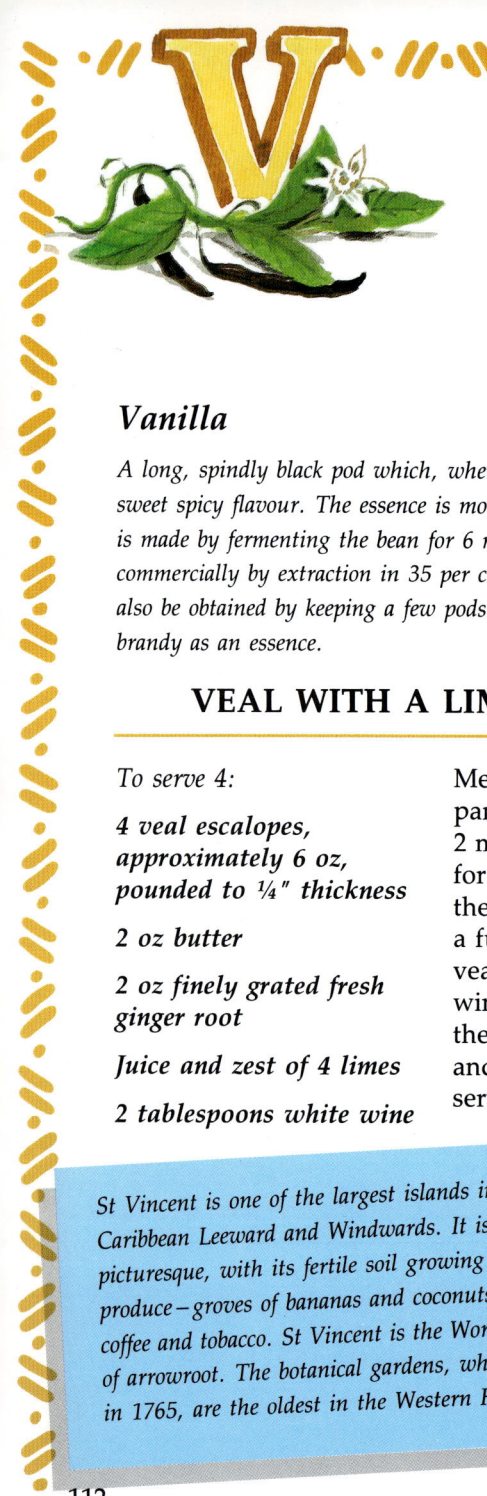

Vanilla

A long, spindly black pod which, when used whole in milk dishes, imparts a sweet spicy flavour. The essence is more widely used in puddings and cakes. It is made by fermenting the bean for 6 months. The extract is then prepared commercially by extraction in 35 per cent alcohol. A homemade extract can also be obtained by keeping a few pods in brandy and using the flavoured brandy as an essence.

VEAL WITH A LIME-GINGER SAUCE

To serve 4:

4 veal escalopes, approximately 6 oz, pounded to ¼" thickness

2 oz butter

2 oz finely grated fresh ginger root

Juice and zest of 4 limes

2 tablespoons white wine

Melt the butter in a large frying pan and sauté the ginger root for 2 minutes. Add the veal and sauté for 4–5 minutes on each side. Add the lime juice and zest and cook for a further 5 minutes. Remove the veal to a warm dish and add the wine to the pan. Bring the sauce to the boil and simmer until it is thick and syrupy. Pour over the veal and serve immediately.

ST VINCENT

St Vincent is one of the largest islands in this chain of Caribbean Leeward and Windwards. It is breathtakingly picturesque, with its fertile soil growing all manner of produce—groves of bananas and coconuts, plantations of coffee and tobacco. St Vincent is the World's largest producer of arrowroot. The botanical gardens, which were established in 1765, are the oldest in the Western Hemisphere.

VEGETABLE GUMBO

To serve 4:

3 tablespoons butter

2 tablespoons flour

4–6 oz okra, finely sliced

1 medium onion, peeled and chopped

1 stick celery, finely sliced

3 cloves garlic, peeled and minced

4 tomatoes, chopped

1 pint vegetable stock

2 medium carrots, peeled and cut into rounds

Sprig thyme

1 tablespoon freshly chopped parsley

2 bay leaves

Hot sauce to taste

2 teaspoons Worcester sauce

4 oz cooked butter beans

1 medium sweet red pepper, deseeded and chopped

2 corn-on-the-cob, cut into rounds

Melt the butter in a large saucepan and sauté the okra, onion, celery and garlic for 2–3 minutes. Add the tomatoes and flour and cook for 1 minute. Add the stock slowly, stirring to form a sauce. Add the carrots, herbs, hot sauce and Worcester sauce. Stir well and cook for 5 minutes, then add the butter beans, red pepper and corn and simmer until the carrots are cooked. Serve hot.

VIRGIN GORDA

Over a century ago Virgin Gorda boasted a large population and centre of commerce; over 400 years ago the Spanish mined copper, gold and silver at Coppermine Point. Today the island is very popular with charter boats and tourists due to the relative abundance of yacht clubs and marinas. The Baths, a geological curiosity, are huge round boulders forming natural swimming pools and caves.

WEST INDIAN SWIZZLE

To serve 1:

½ tablespoon brown sugar

2 oz soda water

Dash of Angostura bitters

2 oz dark West Indian rum

Plenty of crushed ice

Place all the ingredients in a tall glass and swizzle around with a stick to froth. Serve immediately.

Yams

Yams are a staple starchy root vegetable of similar importance to the West Indians as potatoes are to the British. They can be of hard or soft texture after cooking – the hard ones are preferable for salads while the softer ones are often used in soups or as an accompaniment to meat dishes.

YAM SALAD

To serve 8:

1½ lbs yam

2 dill pickles, chopped

3 hard-boiled eggs, peeled and roughly chopped

3 tomatoes, diced

6 green onions, finely chopped

2 celery stalks, finely sliced

3 oz cashew nuts

1 tablespoon freshly chopped parsley

Dressing:
5 tablespoons mayonnaise

4 tablespoons sour cream

1 teaspoon Dijon mustard

1 tablespoon white wine vinegar

Salt and pepper to taste

Combine all the ingredients for the dressing and set aside. Place the unpeeled yams in a large saucepan, cover with water and bring to the boil. Cook for approximately 20–30 minutes until tender, drain, and when cool enough peel and cut into 1" chunks. Place the yam in a large serving bowl, coat with the dressing, mixing gently. Add all the other ingredients and mix. Cover and chill for at least 1 hour before serving.

YELLOWBIRD

To serve 1:

1½ oz dark rum

1 oz orange juice

1 oz pineapple juice

½ oz banana liqueur

Plenty of crushed ice

Place all the ingredients in a tall glass and stir well to blend. Use a cocktail stick with slices of banana, chunks of pineapple, sections of orange and cherries to garnish.

SUGGESTED MENUS

DINNERS

Avocado and basil soup page 3

Fresh swordfish steak
with lime butter page 51

Pigeon peas and rice page 95

Mango icecream page 79

Marinated conch salad page 39

Chicken breast stuffed with banana
in a mango sauce page 26

Steamed sweet potatoes page 106

Ginger and papaya cocktail page 63

Chilled cucumber soup page 44

Creole prawns
in potato straw baskets page 90

Lemon and garlic rice page 95

Banana flambé page 10

Clams
with spicy bread stuffing page 35

Caribbean roast pork page 89

Sautéed breadfruit

Papaya mousse page 85

Spicy eggplant salad page 50

Jerked pork chops page 68

Christophene au gratin page 33

Tropical fresh fruit salad page 110

LUNCHES

Lobster and avocado salad
with garlic bread page 73

Pumpkin and ginger soufflé page 93

Carrot and ginger soup page 21

Bean and cashew nut salad page 13

Banana cream pie page 10

Chicken, avocado and mango salad
with lime-hazelnut dressing page 29

Cornbread muffins page 42

Coconut icecream page 36

Spicy meatballs
with garlic and dill dip page 81

Green salad

Passion fruit fool page 86

Conch fritters
with a piquant tomato sauce page 38

Hearts of palm salad page 65

Mango cheesecake page 77

INDEX

APPETIZERS AND SALADS

Avocado and crab salad with piquant tomato sauce 4
Avocado and papaya salad 6
Avocado lime mousse with chutney chicken salad 5
Avocado with spinach and garlic mayonnaise 6
Barbecued chicken wings 25
Bean and cashew nut salad 13
Caribbean chicken salad 22
Chicken sate 27
Chicken, avocado and mango salad with lime-hazelnut dressing 29
Chilled chicken paprica 31
Clams with spicy bread stuffing 35
Fish balls with mint dip 54
Hearts of palm salad 65
Lobster avocado salad 73
Marinated conch salad 39
Saltfish buljol 100
Spicy eggplant salad 50
Yam salad 115

AVOCADO

Avocado and basil soup 3
Avocado and crab salad with piquant tomato sauce 4
Avocado and papaya salad 6
Avocado lime mousse with chutney chicken salad 5
Avocado with spinach and garlic mayonnaise 6
Chicken, avocado and mango salad with lime-hazelnut dressing 29
Lobster avocado salad 73
Tropical fresh fruit salad 110

BANANA

Banana bread 8
Banana coconut pudding 9
Banana cream pie 10
Banana diaquiri 45
Banana flambé 10
Caribbean banana soup 12
Chicken breasts stuffed with banana in a mango sauce 26
Chicken Surinam 31
Cinnamon chicken with plantains 24
Fruit sorbet 59
Pan-fried honey bananas 11
Peanut and banana punch 87
Sautéed bananas with coconut cream 9
Tropical fresh fruit salad 110

BEEF, PORK AND LAMB

Caribbean beef 14
Caribbean roast pork 89

Jerked pork chops 68
Roast leg of lamb with garlic and guava glaze 72
Spicy lamb stew 71
Spicy meatballs with garlic dill dip 81
Spicy meat patties 82
Veal with lime-ginger sauce 112
West Indian beef 15

BEVERAGES

Banana diaquiri 45
Cream punch 44
Ginger beer 60
Lime diaquiri 45
Lime squash 72
Peanut and banana punch 87
Pina colada 87
Rum punch 96
Sorrel drink and rum 106
West Indian swizzle 114
Yellowbird 116

BREADS

Banana bread 8
Coconut bread 37
Cornbread 42
Dumplings 47
Ginger bread 61
Roti bread 96

BREADFRUIT

Breadfruit baked whole 16
Breadfruit with garlic butter 16

BUTTERNUT

Baked butternut squash with cinnamon 17
Butternut squash casserole 19
Curried cream of butternut and leek soup 18

CARIBBEAN INGREDIENTS

Ackee 1
Allspice 2
Breadfruit 16
Butternut 17
Barbecue 11
Callaloo 20
Cassava 21
Christophene 33
Cinnamon 35
Cloves 35
Coconut milk 35
Conch 37
Diaquiri 45
Eddo 48
Eggplant 48
Figs 51

Fish 51
Genips 60
Ginger 60
Guava 64
Hot peppers 65
Jerk 68
Lime juice 72
Mace 76
Mango 76
Nutmeg 83
Okra 84
Papaya 85
Passion fruit 85
Pepperpot 87
Pineapple 88
Plantains 89
Pumpkin 92
Rice 94
Saltfish 98
Sorrel 105
Soursop 106
Sweet potato 106
Tamarind 109
Turmeric 111
Vanilla 112
Yams 115

CHICKEN

Avocado lime mousse with chutney chicken
salad 5
Barbecued chicken wings 25
Caribbean chicken salad 22
Chicken, avocado and mango salad with
lime-hazelnut dressing 29
Chicken breasts stuffed with banana in
a mango sauce 26
Chicken pelau 32
Chicken sate 27
Chicken Surinam 31
Chilled chicken paprika 31
Cinnamon chicken with plantains 24
Honey chicken with a lemon and garlic
stuffing 28
Mango chutney chicken 30

CHRISTOPHENE

Christophene and caraway 33
Christophene au gratin 33

COCONUT

Banana coconut pudding 9
Caribbean banana soup 12
Chicken pelau 32
Coconut bread 37
Coconut icecream 36
Coconut rice 94
Fresh coconut milk 36
Fruit sorbet 59
Pina colada 87
Sautéed bananas with coconut cream 9
Shrimp with coconut in garlic butter 105

CONCH

Conch chowder I 40
Conch chowder II 41

Conch fritters 38
Marinated conch salad 39

DESSERTS

Banana coconut pudding 9
Banana cream pie 10
Banana flambé 10
Coconut icecream 36
Fruit sorbet 59
Ginger and papaya cocktail 63
Guava cheese 64
Lime delight 73
Mango cheesecake 77
Mango sherbet 79
Pan-fried honey bananas 11
Papaya mousse 85
Passion fruit fool 86
Pineapple flambé 88
Pumpkin and ginger soufflé 93
Sautéed bananas with coconut cream 9
Soursop cream 106
Sweet potato pudding 108
Tropical fresh fruit salad 110

FISH

Fish balls with mint dip 54
Fish curry with eggplant and tomato 57
Fish with creamy lobster sauce 53
Fish with fresh chillis and tamarind 58
Fish with green peppercorn sauce 52
Fish with white cucumber sauce 52
Saltfish and ackee 99
Saltfish buljol 100
Seafood gumbo 101
Shark fillet with pepper sauce 55
West Indian fish soup 56

GINGER

Carrot and ginger soup 21
Ginger beer 60
Ginger bread 61
Ginger and papaya cocktail 63
Mango chutney 78
Pumpkin and ginger soufflé 93
Shrimp in a lime-ginger sauce 105
Veal with a lime-ginger glaze 112

ISLANDS

Anguilla 2
Antigua 2
Barbados 11
Barbuda 8
St Barts 13
Dominica 46
St Eustatius 50
Grenada 62
The Grenadines 63
Guadeloupe 64
Jamaica 67
St John 68
St Kitts 70
St Lucia 73
Market scenes 80
St Martin 77
Martinique 80

119

Montserrat 81
Nevis 83
Redonda 94
Saba 98
St Thomas 110
Tortola 111
Trinidad and Tobago 111
Virgin Gorda 114
St Vincent 112

LOBSTER

Lobster avocado salad 73
Lobster with garlic or lime butter 74
Lobster thermidor 75

MANGO

Chicken, avodaco and mango salad with lime-hazelnut dressing 29
Chicken breasts stuffed with banana in a mango sauce 26
Fruit sorbet 59
Mango cheesecake 77
Mango chutney 78
Mango chutney chicken 30
Mango fool 78
Mango icecream 79
Mango sherbet 79
Tropical fresh fruit salad 110

PINEAPPLE

Caribbean chicken salad 22
Pina colada 87
Pineapple flambé 88
Scalloped pineapple and corn 88
Tropical fresh fruit salad 110

PAPAYA

Avocado and papaya salad 6
Ginger and papaya cocktail 63
Hot sauce 66
Papaya mousse 85
Tropical fresh fruit salad 110

PUMPKIN

Pumpkin and ginger soufflé 93
Pumpkin soup 92
Seafood gumbo 101

SEAFOOD

Chilled shrimp bisque 102
Clams with spicy bread stuffing 35
Conch fritters 38
Creole prawns served in a potato straw basket 90
Curried shrimp soup 103
Fish curry with eggplant and tomato 57
Fish with creamy lobster sauce 53
Fish with fresh chillis and tamarind 58
Fish with green peppercorn sauce 52
Fish with white cucumber sauce 52
Lobster avocado salad 73
Lobster thermidor 75

Lobster with garlic or lime butter 74
Saltfish and ackee 90
Saltfish buljol 100
Seafood gumbo 101
Shark fillet with pepper sauce 55
Shrimp in lime ginger sauce 105
Shrimp sautéed in garlic butter 104
Shrimp with coconut in garlic butter 105

SHRIMP AND PRAWNS

Chilled shrimp bisque 102
Creole prawns served in a potato straw basket 90
Curried shrimp soup 103
Seafood gumbo 101
Shrimp sautéed in garlic butter 104
Shrimp with coconut in garlic butter 105
Shrimp with lime ginger sauce 105
West Indian fish soup 56

SOUPS

Avocado and basil soup 3
Caribbean banana soup 12
Callaloo soup 20
Carrot and ginger soup 21
Chilled cucumber soup 44
Chilled shrimp bisque 102
Conch chowder I 40
Conch chowder II 41
Cream of sweet potato soup 107
Curried cream of butternut and leek soup 18
Curried shrimp soup 103
Pumpkin soup 92
Seafood gumbo 101
Vegetable gumbo 113
West Indian fish soup 56

SWEET POTATO

Candied sweet potato 107
Cream of sweet potato soup 107
Sweet potato pudding 108
West Indian fish soup 56

VEGETABLES AND SIDE DISHES

Ackee, mushroom and cheese soufflé 1
Baked butternut squash with cinnamon 17
Barbecued kidney beans 70
Breadfruit baked whole 16
Breadfruit with garlic butter 16
Butternut squash casserole 19
Candied sweet potato 107
Christophene and caraway 33
Christophene au gratin 33
Coconut rice 94
Corn fritters 43
Eggplant creole 49
Hot sauce 66
Lemon and garlic rice 95
Mango chutney 78
Okra creole 84
Rice and peas 95
Roti bread 96
Scalloped pineapple and corn 88